enjoying
WINE

enjoying
WINE

A complete guide to understanding,
choosing, and drinking wine

Chris Losh

RYLAND
PETERS
& SMALL

LONDON NEW YORK

First published in the United States in 2006 by Ryland Peters & Small
519 Broadway, 5th Floor
New York, NY 10012
www.rylandpeters.com

10 9 8 7 6 5 4

Senior Designers Carl Hodson, Catherine Griffin

Senior Editor Clare Double

Recipe Editor Rachel Lawrence

Production Simon Walsh

Picture Research Emily Westlake

Art Director Anne-Marie Bulat

Publishing Director Alison Starling

Printed in China

Library of Congress Cataloging-in-Publication Data
Losh, Chris.
  Enjoying wine : a complete guide to understanding, choosing, and drinking wine / Chris Losh. – 1st U.S. ed.
     p. cm.
  Includes index.
  ISBN-13: 978-1-84597-238-7
  ISBN-10: 1-84597-238-4
  1. Wine and wine making. I. Title.
  TP548.L675 2006
  641.2'2–dc22
                                    2006014511

Conversion chart

Volume equivalents:

American	Metric	Imperial
¼ cup	60 ml	2 fl.oz.
⅓ cup	75 ml	2½ fl.oz.
½ cup	125 ml	4 fl.oz.
⅔ cup	150 ml	5 fl.oz. (¼ pint)
¾ cup	175 ml	6 fl.oz.
1 cup	250 ml	8 fl.oz.

Weight equivalents:

Imperial	Metric	Imperial	Metric
1 oz.	30 g	8 oz. (½ lb.)	225 g
2 oz.	55 g	10 oz.	280 g
3 oz.	85 g	12 oz.	350 g
4 oz.	115 g	14 oz.	400 g
5 oz.	140 g	16 oz. (1 lb.)	450 g
6 oz.	175 g		

Oven temperatures:

140°C	275°F	Gas 1
150°C	300°F	Gas 2
170°C	325°F	Gas 3
180°C	350°F	Gas 4
190°C	375°F	Gas 5
200°C	400°F	Gas 6
230°C	450°F	Gas 8

contents

Wine is the greatest **affordable luxury** on the planet. It turns a Sunday roast into a **banquet**, transforms a bowl of Wednesday-night pasta from simple refueling into a proper meal, and even adds a touch of **magic** to an evening in front of the TV.

introduction

Wine encourages us to sit down and talk to our friends and family, to take our foot off the gas and give ourselves some much-needed down time. It's a social lubricant, a massage for the palate, and a long hot bath for the soul, all in one.

Sure, you might be saying, but it's also enormously complicated. And with hundreds of grape varieties, thousands of producers, and millions of bottles to choose from, you'd be right to an extent. It's the reason we so often fall back on boring old wines that we've had 50 times before, or get it wrong when we do branch out and try something unusual.

Yet for all that, it doesn't take much to get a handle on wine. You don't, for instance, need to stuff your head with the names of zillions of French châteaux or memorize every tweak and twiddle of how a wine is made to improve your hit rate. All you need is enough basic knowledge to get you started and a willingness to go out and explore.

The second part is up to you, but the getting started bit is where this book comes in. Within these pages, I've sifted the mountains of weird, complicated, and usually unnecessary information that surrounds wine, and left you with the easy-to-remember, important stuff that will actually make a difference to what you buy and how you drink it.

Above all, I hope I've also done it in a way that makes it obvious that if wine is about anything it's about having fun. This book isn't going to give you chapter and verse on the French appellation system or the history of grape-growing in California because, frankly, unless you're a wine geek, that stuff's pretty boring. Instead, I've concentrated on how the different grape varieties taste, what the different countries do well, which wines go best with which occasions, and how to get the right bottle for whatever you happen to be eating. In other words, practical, no-nonsense information that will help you on a day-to-day level.

Wine might be a big, potentially baffling subject, but a little knowledge goes a very long way toward demystifying it, and if you use this book as your guide, you'll soon be buying and drinking it with confidence.

So read *Enjoying Wine* in the spirit it was written: with a glass by your side and a spirit of adventure. May you taste, learn, savor—and, most of all, enjoy!

understanding WINE

Ever wondered why the same wine tastes so different from bottles produced in different countries? This chapter explains how soil, climate, and other factors affect wine's flavor.

the grape variety

Have you heard of Cabernet Sauvignon, Chardonnay, and Merlot? They're not places, wine regions, or brand names, they're grape varieties–and they're some of the biggest factors that influence what a wine tastes like. Think of it like this: in the same way that you get different breeds of dog or different species of flower, so you also get different types of grape.

And just as a Rottweiler is different from a greyhound, yet they are both dogs, or a daffodil is different from a tulip, yet they are both flowers, so a Cabernet Sauvignon is different from a Merlot and a Chardonnay is different from a Viognier, yet they are all grape varieties (also called varietals).

There are hundreds of them out there, and they all have their own characteristics. Some reds are heavy and chunky, some soft and round, while some are so light they can be chilled and drunk with fish. Whites,

meanwhile, run from delicate and fragrant to so big and solid they're almost a meal in themselves. Some grapes will grow brilliantly in one place, but be unable to produce anything worth drinking in another. Some are tolerant and reliable, others are erratic geniuses capable both of hitting the heights and plumbing the depths from one year to the next.

All of this is what makes wine so interesting and, to the uninitiated, confusing. But fortunately, though there are (honestly!) thousands of grape varieties out

there, the vast majority of wines nowadays are probably made from no more than about 20, all of which are covered in this book.

Some wines are made from just one grape variety—a 100% Cabernet Sauvignon, for instance. Others are a blend of different grapes, where the winemaker has attempted to create a wine that is greater than the sum of its parts by mixing several varietals together—say, Grenache/Shiraz/Mourvèdre. In many of Europe's classic wine regions this has been common for centuries, but now it's growing in popularity in the New World, too.

The main thing is not to be daunted by the choice available. If you were planting a garden, you wouldn't fill it with only one type of flower, so when it comes to wine, don't limit yourself to two or three tried and tested favorites, either!

the climate

Ever wondered why some countries make wine and others don't? Or why some places are famous for making wines from one particular grape and not others? Or even why a Cabernet Sauvignon from California tastes different to one from Bordeaux? A large part of the answer can be summed up in one word: climate. The vine is a pretty tolerant plant (in fact, it's basically a weed) and it will do its best to grow anywhere bar deserts and the Poles.

However, when it comes to producing fruit that is good enough to make into wine, you're looking at an area between 30° and 50° latitude, north and south of the equator. Here, it's not too hot in summer, and cool enough for the vines to get a rest in winter—although if your region is prone to searing heat, strong winds, spring frosts, drought, or rain at the wrong time of year, it's hard to make it commercially viable for wine-growing. This explains why vines aren't grown in, say, high, dry, dusty Mongolia, even though it's at the same latitude as France.

Temperature is probably the most obvious climatic factor affecting a wine's flavor. Vines in a hot place will give super-ripe grapes (which means plenty of alcohol) and wines that are big and blowsy. Those from a cooler area are more subtle, but can be thin or unripe in the hands of less talented growers.

The perfect climate for really great wine (as opposed to just good wine) is somewhere it's possible to ripen the grapes—but only just. The problem with these so-called marginal climates is that they can, by their very nature, be unreliable: great one year, rotten the next. It's why great Bordeaux or (especially) Burgundy can be magnificent, but close to undrinkable in really bad years, while wines from Australia's sun-drenched Riverland area are decent year in, year out, but not terribly exciting.

The Riverland, in fact, wouldn't be able to make wine at all without irrigation. Pumping water into vines has allowed all sorts of places (particularly in the New World) to make wine that would probably have been considered too dry for it 50 years ago. But while climate remains relatively steady, weather remains gloriously unpredictable. Hot countries can have cool years, and marginal climates that struggle to ripen grapes at all one year can swelter the next. It's why wines can change character from year to year, and it's what makes the topic so interesting. So read on!

Soil might seem an odd thing to get excited about, but if you spend any time with a winemaker, you can pretty much guarantee that before long they'll start talking animatedly about the land on which their grapes are grown. It's a good point. You might think that soil is soil is soil, but in fact, in any vineyard there can be dozens of different soil types, with varying percentages of clay, minerals, sand, stones, and the like.

the soil

Some soils are rich in nutrients, others are poor; some drain well, others hold the water; some are full of stones or pebbles, others light and silty.

Fine, you might say, but does it make a difference? Scientists have carried out tests and say that, beyond their ability to hold water (or not), it shouldn't. Practical experience suggests that the pointy-heads should spend less time in the lab and more time with a glass in their hand. I've tried half a dozen wines from the same company, grown in vineyards no more than a few miles apart, made identically, all of which taste different. Not chalk-and-cheese different, but certainly Stilton and Monterey Jack different.

Admittedly, slight differences in climate from one place to another (even just a few miles apart) can have an effect, particularly if the land is sloping (and so toward the sun or away from the sun). But

winemakers the world over insist that the main reason for the taste differences is the land itself.

The Europeans (and especially the French) have always thought like this. It explains their emotional attachment to plots of earth, and also why the best word to sum up the whole concept is a French one. *Terroir* (pronounced "tair-wahr") is the word used all over the wine world to describe a site's characteristics: its temperature, rainfall, drainage, sunlight, and—perhaps most important of all—its soil.

But it's no longer just Europeans who are buying into the whole terroir thing. Well-educated, techno-literate 20-something winemakers from all over the world think more and more that the land holds the key. Winemakers don't come over all gooey when talking about the latest piece of technological wizardry in their winery, but they do when they talk about their vineyards. "Man," they'll say, "that's a great piece of land. Unbelievable terroir..." And they'll be off again on a misty-eyed monologue about soil.

the winery

The biggest winery I've ever seen (in California) was the size of a small gasoline refinery. The smallest (in France) would have just about fit into my garage, and had a staff of two. One had **computerized wizardry** and men in overalls; the other looked as if it had barely changed in a century and had **muddy boots** lined up at the door.

Yet both had the same purpose: to turn grapes into wine. A winery isn't much more than a processing plant—a kind of wine factory. But it's also the place that alchemizes the grape into liquid poetry.

Winemakers are the chief magicians of this arcane process, but they view their job not as magic, but as damage limitation—allowing the character that is locked up in the grapes to reach the bottle with the minimum of interference from them. They are fond of saying that you can't make good wine with bad grapes, but you can make bad wine with good grapes.

Basically, winemaking is quite simple: grapes are crushed and their juice is fermented, turning the sugar into alcohol. However, within this millennia-old process, there are hundreds of technical factors that affect how a wine will turn out: what temperature you ferment at, how long you leave red grapes in

contact with their skins, and whether you want to add (or soften) acidity. These all have a great bearing on the final wine, and that's before you get into whether a wine is fermented or aged in barrel (see page 18) and how the various factors are blended together.

Ah, yes—blending. Even a wine that is 100% one grape variety is probably going to be made of grapes from different vineyards. It's up to the winemaker to decide first how he makes each "parcel," then in what percentages he wants to blend them: a bit like trying to put together a liquid jigsaw puzzle using your nose.

Difficult, in other words, and made more so by the fact that most of the big decisions need to be taken quickly, at a time when the winemaker is exhausted. Wines ferment 24 hours a day, so during vintage the winemaker survives on coffee, adrenaline, and limited sleep. It's a tough job, but someone has to do it...

the barrels

Most red wines and a fair percentage of whites will spend time "in wood"– which usually means either aging or fermenting in an oak barrel. Wines were originally kept in barrels as a means of storage, either for journeys or at the winery. Nowadays, storage is in stainless-steel tanks.

Today, barrels are used purely for the style they impart to the wine. The classiest are made of French oak, but they're expensive, so some wineries use American oak barrels either as well as or instead of them. Typically, a French oak barrel imparts broad, toasty, spicy flavors to the wine; American oak barrels have more upfront vanilla and clove characteristics. Wineries on a budget go for the "aged in oak" effect by putting "teabags" of oak chips or big wooden staves in the wine as it rests.

Overt flavor differences aren't the only reason to put wine in barrels, however. The time a wine spends in wood allows it to mellow, smoothing rough edges and allowing the wine to age gracefully. An obvious example is a Riojan Gran Reserva, which spends years in old barrels (and then in the bottle) before it's released, and is super-smooth as a result. But it doesn't taste heavily of wood; not every barrel affects a wine the same way. A big barrel has less effect than a small one, since less wine is in contact with the wood.

Likewise, an old barrel won't impart overt "woody" flavors to a wine, while a few months in a brand-new barrel will have a marked influence on a wine's flavor. Balancing the amount of wood in a wine is a key part of the winemaker's job. In the 1990s, many (particularly Australian) Chardonnays tasted more of wood than wine, but this is no longer the case.

Not all wines spend time in oak. Young red wines (like Beaujolais Nouveau) and aromatic whites like Riesling, Muscadet, and Soave rarely go into barrel.

In wine, age matters. Classic old vintages are spoken about reverentially, while winemakers talk about "old vines" with the sort of affection usually reserved for childhood friends and pets. But does it matter whether the fruit in a wine has come from vines that are five years old or fifty?

vine age and wine age

The answer, emphatically, is "yes." Young vines are like small children: they have lots of enthusiasm, but not a lot of focus. They produce large numbers of grapes, but not much in the way of character.

Old vines, meanwhile, are like those toothless old men you find sitting on a bench. They don't produce a lot, but what nuggets they do give you tend to be worth the wait. Old vines produce a lot less fruit than younger vines, but the grapes they can be bothered to ripen are far more concentrated, with greater depth of flavor and personality, than those produced by immature vines. That's why some bottles actually mention "old vines" (*vieilles vignes*/*viñas viejas* in French and Spanish) on the label.

Vines in Europe tend to be older than those in the New World, most of whose vineyards have been planted (or replanted) in the last 30 years. In France, a 30-year-old vine would barely be worth a mention; in places like Chile's Maipo Valley or New Zealand's Marlborough, it would be a tourist attraction.

Just as vine age matters, so does wine age. The vast majority of wines nowadays are made "ready to drink," and don't benefit much from being left for a few years. But there are some wine styles (particularly pricier European wines from places like Bordeaux and Tuscany) that don't just benefit from a bit of cellar time, but actually require it to make them drinkable.

That's because they are so concentrated when young that they're inaccessible. These wines are designed to be drunk years down the line. When they're young, their tannins are enormous and their flavors in a tight little ball that makes them an effort rather than a pleasure to drink. They need to open out, and that only happens if the wine is left to age (in the right conditions—see page 226) for a few years.

With time, the tannins soften, the fruit opens out, and the wine starts to develop fascinating "secondary characteristics" that move beyond the simply fruity and into something altogether more complex.

That said, there are few things more disappointing than a really good bottle of wine that's been left too long and is well over the hill. If in doubt, pull the cork!

understanding wine labels

Using your eyes to decide what your palate might enjoy is, on one level, about as illogical as trying to choose a new suit by sniffing it! But even pretty poor wine labels give you enough to allow you to make at least a half-informed decision on the wine. Most wine labels will tell you:

Who made it

Picking wine can be a gamble. If you find a wine you really like—or don't like—make a note for next time.

Where it's from

After reading this book you should know more about countries' key regions (or appellations). Some labels tell you the sub-zone within an appellation. California and Burgundy are appellations; Napa Valley and the Côte de Beaune, sub-zones within them. *Appellation Meursault Contrôlée* or *Denominación de Origen Rioja* means the wine has come from that recognized region and is made in accordance with its regulations.

What it's made of

Labeling wines by grape variety is a practice introduced by the New World over the last 30 years. Now even European countries who don't traditionally label their wine varietally will often tell you what it's made from on the back label. If not, the appellation will usually give you a clue. For instance, Chablis is

Chardonnay, red Burgundy is Pinot Noir, and Chianti is made from Sangiovese. (More in the next chapter.)

Whether it's oaked

"Reserve" on a label usually means a wine has spent time aging in barrel. Wineries are often quite specific on the back label. Three months in oak isn't long; 18 months is. *Barrique* in French (*barrica* in Spanish, *botte* in Italian) means "barrel" and means the wine's been in oak. If it says new oak, the effect will be stronger.

What level it's at

Appellation Contrôlée (*Denominación de Origen* in Spain, *Denominazione di Origine* in Italy) is strictly controlled. Wines must come from designated grapes with low yields, grown in a specific area. *Vin de Pays* (*Vino de la Tierra* in Spain, *IGT* in Italy) is wine from a specified region, but with higher yields; more grapes are permitted. *Vin de Table* (*Vino de Mesa* in Spain, *Vino da Tavola* in Italy) is table wine. With no grape restrictions or geographical limit, it allows high yields.

where
WINE comes from

Wine is grown and made all over the world, from chilly
Champagne country in northern France to California's
sun-baked Central Valley. This chapter is your guided tour.

france

Ask anyone to mention the country that they most associate with wine, and more often than not they'll say France. From images of the gnarled peasant tending his vines to grand old châteaux, from magnums of bubbly at society dinners to tables strewn with bottles in smoky brasseries, *vin* is as much a part of the French way of life as the Gallic shrug. And, while France has lost market share to the New World, it's still the most powerful wine-producing country on the planet. Some of this influence is down to sheer volume, but most of France's power stems from her iconic producers and regions.

In fact, it was to protect the good name of places like Bordeaux that the first wine *appellation contrôlée* was set up over 150 years ago. Basically, an appellation formalizes a wine region's boundaries and dictates what grape varieties can be grown there. There are dozens of them all over France, from Champagne in the chilly north to Bandol in the foothills of the Pyrenees.

Hundreds of years of people debating the best places to grow certain grapes, and an organized system to encourage it, would be worthless without a staggeringly good geography. The French often like to claim that God is one of them, and when it comes to wine they might just, infuriatingly, have a point.

France, after all, has everything. It has mountains in the east and seas to the north, west, and south; its landscape is liberally crossed with majestic rivers, cutting swathes through rolling hillsides; its regional climates veer from cool and damp to hot and dry. Put all this together and you have a blueprint for growing pretty much any grape you choose. It's the reason why, despite increased competition, France still sets the quality benchmark for Cabernet Sauvignon, Merlot, Chardonnay, Pinot Noir, Gewürztraminer, sparkling wines, and, arguably, Syrah and Sauvignon Blanc.

BORDEAUX

Probably the most famous wine-producing region in the world, Bordeaux lies about three-quarters of the way down France, just in from the Atlantic coast, spreading out all around the city of the same name.

To the west, near the sea, lies the "left bank" (so called because it's left of the Gironde estuary) and the stony, gravelly soils of the Médoc. This is the

Cabernet Sauvignon capital of the world and home to four of the five super-famous first growths: Châteaux Lafite, Latour, Margaux, and Mouton Rothschild.

In good years, Médoc appellations like Pauillac, St-Julien, St-Estèphe, and Margaux make wines of a depth, concentration, and perfumed finesse that the rest of the world can only dream of. Founded on Cabernet Sauvignon's power and tannin, these are wines for long-term aging, not drinking young.

To the south are Graves and Pessac-Léognan (where you'll find both the region's best white wines and the other first growth, Haut-Brion), while in the southeastern corner is Sauternes, the region that makes the most elegant and characterful sweet wines in the world from Sémillon and Sauvignon Blanc.

To the east and north of the city, it's vines, vines, and more vines. It doesn't make for the most exciting landscape photography, but it's the place to go if you want to find names like Pétrus and Le Pin, the most expensive wines on the planet. In these "right bank" Bordeaux appellations of St-Émilion and Pomerol, the châteaux are smaller and quirkier, and the key grapes are not Cabernet Sauvignon (as you'll find on the left bank), but Merlot and Cabernet Franc, which prefer the cooler, water-retaining clay soils.

In fact, the mix of grape varietals in Bordeaux is one of the keys to the region. This is not only because of the complementary way in which the various grapes are blended together, but because in just about every vintage, the weather will have suited one of the grape types and one of the regions, meaning that there will be some good—and even very good—wines made.

BURGUNDY

You might think that because Burgundy only has two main grape varieties (Bordeaux, for instance, has four times that), it would be easy to understand. And on one hand, it's comforting to know that a Bourgogne Rouge is made from Pinot Noir, and a white from Chardonnay. But nothing in Burgundy is quite that simple.

For starters there are thousands of small producers, who often own tiny plots of vineyard all over the region. Some of these growers can make good wine from unpromising areas, while others manage to make dross from great sites.

Then there's the fact that the appellation itself is split up into five different levels of classification, from the tiny "Grands Crus" (applied to specific hallowed vineyards) at the top, through Village appellations, to the generic "Burgundy" appellation, which can take in wine grown anywhere in the delineated region.

It's all very confusing—and it's not helped by the fact that Burgundy has a pretty marginal climate. It's about halfway down the eastern third of the country, running in a straggly north–south strip, and in cold years its wines can be quite austere. In fact, Chablis, at the northern edge of the appellation, is famous for its steely character. Hot years aren't much good either, though, because then the wines lack true Burgundian character and finesse.

So why bother? Because when Burgundy gets it right, it gets it spectacularly right. Its top whites are the most extraordinary expressions of Chardonnay anywhere in the world, and there isn't a winemaker alive who wouldn't sell his soul for the chance to make a red Burgundy from a top vineyard in a great year.

Drinking Burgundian Pinot Noir is like listening to Mozart or Billie Holiday—it's genius that carries its

beauty effortlessly and makes the hairs stand up on the back of your neck. Other places in the world make good (and sometimes very good) Pinot Noir, but nowhere else can touch greatness with this most temperamental of grapes.

CHAMPAGNE

Champagne is a long way north, in the cold, flat, wind-blasted fields to the east of Paris, between the French capital and Germany. But this non-tourist-friendly climate is important. Even when the grapes struggle to ripeness in early autumn, they still have plenty of acidity—which is exactly what you need to make good fizz. The "base wine" for champagne is gum-strippingly undrinkable, but it's what gives champagne its freshness, and distinguishes it from many versions in the (warmer) New World. Read more on the world's favorite sparkler on pages 116–120.

THE RHÔNE

Just below Beaujolais in the southern reaches of Burgundy, we run into the Côtes du Rhône. The north is the home of some of the world's best Syrah/Shiraz, from places like Hermitage and Côte Rôtie. These great wines, of complexity and elegance that will age for years, are thought by many to be far better value for money than their aristocratic cousins in Bordeaux.

Farther south, in the heartland of the Côtes du Rhône, the wines are typically Grenache-based, often with Syrah, Mourvèdre, and Cinsaut. The latter two rarely make wines on their own, but are useful blending components here. The best examples are typically ripe, round, and well-fruited with plenty of power and character, usually at a pretty good price.

Also in the southern Rhône is Châteauneuf-du-Pape, whose heavy bottles with their embossed coat of arms are as chunky and instantly recognizable as the big, powerful Grenache-based wines themselves.

THE LOIRE

The mighty Loire, ambling its way in from the Atlantic coast toward Paris, before changing its mind and heading southward for hundreds of miles, is home to some of France's best white wines.

Muscadet, near the coast, is pleasant and gluggable rather than exciting, but the thrilling, flinty minerality of Sauvignon Blanc from Sancerre, or the green pepper, grass, and gooseberry flavors of a Pouilly-Fumé version, are genuine pleasures. So, too, are the lush, exotic Chenin Blancs from Vouvray.

As for reds, it's too cool this far north for most varieties, though Cabernet Francs from Chinon and Bourgueil manage to be both lively and fruity, and also able to age for many years.

ALSACE

This is the most northerly of France's wine regions but, protected by the hulking Vosges Mountains, it is one of the driest, too. White wines rule, with excellent Rieslings and Pinot Gris. It's also indisputably the best place in the world for the exotic, Turkish-delight-scented Gewürztraminer grape.

THE SOUTH

The vast chugging engine of French wine, the Languedoc produces massive amounts of the stuff every year. Quality used to be patchy, but it has improved, and some of these mostly Grenache/Syrah/Mourvèdre/Carignan-based wines are now justifiably expensive. There is good value for money to be had if you know where to look.

italy

Italy is the biggest wine-producing country in the world, and a hard one to get a handle on. There are scores of appellations (or *denominazione* as they're called), thousands of producers, not many big brands, and (like much of the Old World) a general aversion to varietal labeling. In any case, putting grape varietals on the label wouldn't help much in Italy.

The country doesn't go in much for "international" varieties like Chardonnay or Merlot, and nearly all the grapes here are only found in any number in Italy itself. Ever heard of Sangiovese, Garganega, or Corvina? Probably not, but I bet you know Chianti, Soave, and Valpolicella, which is what they each make. So yes, Italy is confusing, but it also makes wines that are genuinely different—sometimes thrillingly so—and is worth investigating with an open mind.

PIEMONTE

This region in Italy's northwestern corner contains dozens of different appellations, many of them utterly forgettable. But it's also home to the big guns Barolo and Barbaresco. Made from the sulky, late-ripening Nebbiolo grape, Barolo, when it's bad, is tough and charmless. However, when it's good, it's majestic, all truffles, tar, and violets, and capable of long aging. Perfect for drinking with rare beef.

CHIANTI

Head south of Florence through the rolling countryside toward Siena and you will find yourself in Italy's best-known wine region. Chianti is all about red wine, which in this case means Sangiovese, a sun-loving grape that luxuriates on its south-facing slopes

like a Florida retiree on a sunlounger. The only problem here is that the wide variety of microclimates provided by the assorted slopes, valleys, rivers, and soils—not to mention the thousands of individual growers—means wines that vary enormously in style from light and zippy to serious and tannic. Generally, quality is way up on 20 years ago.

"Supertuscans" like Sassicaia or Tignanello are a blend of Cabernet Sauvignon and Sangiovese: they mean high quality and high prices.

THE VENETO

The slopes around Verona (not far from Venice) are famed for making wines of easy-drinking gluggability. Soave (made from Garganega) can be either boring or charming, depending on who's made it, while the light Valpolicella is its red equivalent. Upfront, easy, and cherry-fruited, it's a useful light- to medium-bodied red for dishes like turkey or pasta.

THE SOUTH

Weird and wonderful grape varieties flourish in the hot south, with—perhaps surprisingly, given the climate—some interesting whites, too. The most user-friendly wine, though, is the juicy, spicy Primitivo, reckoned to be the same grape as California's Zinfandel.

spain

Spain is the world's third-biggest wine-producing country. Until recently it suffered from a rather fusty, old-fashioned image that it mostly deserved, but the last ten years have seen major modernization.

Like Italy, Spain has a large canon of local grape varieties to play with, and Tempranillo (under its various regional names) is the most popular and the best. Many Spanish regions are now also having real success with the likes of Cabernet Sauvignon and Chardonnay, sometimes on their own and sometimes blended with local grapes to create exciting combinations. Spain, in other words, is a country with energy, vitality, and, when it gets it right, almost unbeatable value for money.

RIOJA

Unquestionably Spain's best-known region, for many wine lovers Rioja is Spain, simple as that. It's in the country's northeast, protected from the cool, damp Atlantic coast 100 miles away by a mountain range.

Bordeaux families came here in the 19th century, when their own vineyards were decimated by phylloxera, and they brought with them the idea of aging wines in barrel that has been so central to Riojan winemaking ever since. Crianzas, Reservas, and Gran Reservas all spend a minimum amount of time aging in barrel and bottle. The wines are typically made from a mixture of Tempranillo, Garnacha (Grenache), and Mazuelo and, soft, silky, and well-fruited, are usually a nailed-down match with lamb.

RIBERA DEL DUERO

To the southwest of Rioja lies Ribera del Duero—for many critics, now the home of Spain's finest red wines. On this high, dry plain, where a short growing season keeps growers on their toes, it's searingly hot during the day and cold at night, giving wines of extraordinary concentration.

WHITE WINES

Spain isn't really known for its whites, but two regions make really good stuff. Rías Baixas, in the cool, damp northwest, does great things with the fleshy, charming Albariño grape, while Rueda regularly turns out excellent aromatic Sauvignon Blancs, often blended with the local Verdejo.

SHERRY

From the Moorish deep south comes one of the wine world's classic drinks. Sherry can be pale or brown, sweet or dry, and ranges in strength from about the same as a table wine to the same as a port. One thing this perennially underrated drink nearly always is, though, is good value for money. Find out more on page 129.

CAVA

Spain's homegrown sparkling wine is a mix of local grapes and, sometimes, Chardonnay. It's not, for the most part, terribly demanding stuff, but it's a good budget fizz, and some of the top examples provide plenty of bang for their buck.

germany

One day the wine-drinking public will wake up to German wine once again. It may be hard to believe now, but a hundred years ago some of the world's **most desirable** and expensive wines came not from France, but her Teutonic neighbor.

Yes, Germany is a pretty cold place to be making wine (which is why there isn't much red wine), but the best vineyards are planted on **steep slopes** around rivers, where they can soak up all the sun that is going.

Key regions
MOSEL-SAAR-RUWER, RHEINGAU, PFALZ, NAHE

These top vineyards still make some magnificently good wines, with a grape that most critics regard as the noblest of all white varietals. Forget Chardonnay and Sauvignon Blanc. If you want a really great white wine, drink Riesling, specifically German Riesling.

If all that's true, why is the country's wine image down in the gutter rather than up in lights? Partly, it's because the best wines tend to have a certain amount of sweetness on the palate, and nowadays most people prefer their wines dry. But mostly it's because for 30 years the country flooded the world with a tidal wave of rotten sugar-water that cost little, tasted of less, and undermined the reputation of an entire industry.

These wines weren't made from Riesling on steep slopes, but from Müller-Thurgau grown on the flat. It had the advantage of being cheap to grow and the slight disadvantage of tasting of zip, zero, nada. It defeated all the good work that decent growers were doing and left German wine as trendy as a purple velour jacket.

If you want to give German wine a go—and you should—then look for a Riesling. If you want something light and bouncy, try one which is labeled Kabinett or Spätlese. Auslese and Trockenbeerenauslese are richer and, often, sweeter. There it is again: the S word. But the joy of German Rieslings is that, even with a little sweetness on the palate, they are never cloying: the grapes' zippy natural acidity sees to that. So they can work with food—summer salads and creamy chicken or pork are good—but they're also an absolute joy to drink on their own: light, full of flavor, fresh, and, crucially if you're bored with Chardonnay, different.

rest of europe

From the shores of the Atlantic to the Black Sea, Europe is covered with vines. Even countries you might not associate with wine often have traditions of vine-growing going back thousands of years.

PORTUGAL

A big wine-producing country, Portugal is probably best known globally for its famous fortified wine, port (see page 126). But it has a sizeable table wine industry as well. The best reds come from the port-producing Douro Valley, made with varieties like Touriga Nacional, Tinta Roriz, and Tinta Francesa, though Cabernet, Chardonnay, et al, are being grown with some success farther south.

GREECE

Look beyond the pine-flavored retsina and you'll find interesting moves afoot in one of the oldest wine-producing countries in the world. You might not have heard of varieties like Xinomavro or Aghiorghitiko, but they can make fantastic wine, and the Greeks are learning how to blend them with international varieties to good effect, too—especially Cabernet Sauvignon.

AUSTRIA

Some of Europe's best white wines, both sweet and dry, come from Austria, but depressingly few make it outside the country's borders. If you get the chance to try an Austrian Riesling, Grüner Veltliner, or sweet wine, take it—they can be sublime.

HUNGARY

Strange local grape varieties and a difficult language have held back Hungarian wine almost as much as the ravages of communism. Now, with better marketing, it's easier to try wines made from the likes of Furmint and Kékfrankos. Bull's Blood is not the force it used to be, but some of the magnificent, luscious Tokaji sweet wines are close to where they were a hundred years ago, when they were known as the "drink of kings."

ROMANIA

Romania produces arguably the best-value Pinot Noir anywhere in the world, but 6,000 years of tradition haven't been enough to counter the chaos that followed the end of communism here.

BULGARIA

Plenty of local grape varieties, but the country's big success has been with grapes like Cabernet Sauvignon. Old, rusting wineries are starting to be replaced, and there are a few good wines coming out of the country now. Certainly cheap...

LEBANON

Some good whites and reds, grown 3,000 feet (900 meters) up in the Bekaa Valley.

ISRAEL

As with Lebanon, altitude in the Golan Heights lowers the high summer temperature. Produces some decent international varietals.

GREAT BRITAIN

Forgettable reds and indifferent whites, but some excellent sparkling wine from a climate and terroir not dissimilar to those of Champagne.

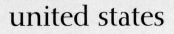

united states

Wine in the United States effectively means California. Although some wine is grown on the eastern side and increasing numbers of decent cooler-climate bottles come from Washington and Oregon (of which more later), the vast majority of America's wine is from the Golden State. Of this, most of California's output comes from the vast, hot, fertile, irrigated plains of the Central Valley—a riot of just about every agricultural crop known to man. In wine terms, it's the equivalent of the south of France, Australia's Riverland, or Spain's La Mancha—an area of big vineyards making lots of wine of, for the most part, no great distinction.

Key regions
CALIFORNIA: NAPA VALLEY, SONOMA, RUSSIAN RIVER VALLEY, CARNEROS, ALEXANDER VALLEY, MENDOCINO, PASO ROBLES
OREGON: WILLAMETTE VALLEY

If you buy a bottle of California wine that doesn't come with a specific regional designation, most or all of it will have come from the Central Valley. Lodi is the one exception to the homogeneity of the Central Valley, producing some very good old-vine Zinfandels, but for the most part, if you're looking for good, interesting wine, you need to leave behind the baking interior and head toward the coast.

Napa Valley, 60 miles north of San Francisco, is arguably the most famous appellation in the whole of the New World, so it comes as something of a surprise that you can drive from one end to the other in about 20 minutes. Many tourists make this run through the summer, though they take days rather than minutes, ambling along Highway 29 and stopping at the myriad wineries that line their route.

Napa's influence, however, is not founded on its size, but on its ability to make great wine, particularly with the Cabernet Sauvignon grape. Napa is not unique in this—great "Cabs" are also made in the neighboring Sonoma and Alexander Valley AVAs (American Viticultural Areas). But still, it's Napa's wines that attract the biggest (often silly) money and whose wineries are the best known, perhaps because they've been making serious wine there

longer than anywhere else in the States. Napa was first planted with quality grapes in the 19th century, when European immigrants (mostly from Germany and Italy) saw its potential and stuck in some European grape varieties.

The Valley boomed, bust during Prohibition, then rose spectacularly from the ashes in the 1960s and 1970s to become the money-stuffed, globally recognized name that it is today.

The key to Napa is the San Francisco Bay at its southern end. The bay lets in cool sea air that funnels its way up the valley, tempering the otherwise relentless sun, while in summer the valley is filled with fog from evening through to mid-morning, which cools the vines further. Thus, Napa has plenty of heat and sun to ripen the grapes, but not so much as to frazzle them, meaning wines with plenty of fruit, but also a bit of structure.

This cool air from the ocean means that there's a huge difference in climate in the 30 miles separating the top end of the Valley from the bottom. Carneros, in the south, is cool, Pinot Noir and Chardonnay country, but as soon as you get to Oakville and Rutherford, less than 20 miles away, sun-loving Cab is king once again. North of here, it is positively hot.

Sonoma, too—Napa's neighbor to the west—has big temperature variations within it; only here there are fewer general rules to hang on to. The fogs and cool Pacific breezes that tumble down the valleys and over the mountain ranges vary from one day, let alone year, to the next, making grape-growing here more complicated and open to chance (so, more European) than in Napa.

If you have to generalize, it's probably safe to say that the northern end is hotter than the southern end, with the fog-filled Russian River Valley home to some of California's best Pinot Noir and white wines. In the Alexander and Dry Creek valleys and Mendocino, as the thermometer rises, you'll find boisterous Zinfandels as well as succulent Cabernets and fewer and fewer white wines.

South of San Francisco, the Central Coast might not have the tourist centers or plethora of famous names of Napa and Sonoma, but there are more and more wineries following the example of Ridge and making excellent wines. Again, it's impossible to generalize, with fog in the valley floors, the influence of altitude on the valley slopes, and sometimes

ferocious sea breezes all being variable balancing factors against the power of the sun. Suffice it to say that there is everything from minerally Chardonnays up near Monterey to big, blockbusting Syrahs, Cabernets, and Zinfandels around Paso Robles and encouraging Pinot Noirs in some of the wind-blown valleys farther south.

Head north of California to Washington and Oregon and it's a different story. The industry here is smaller and more homespun, with the genuinely cooler climate giving wines with a lot less of that big-sun fruit you find farther south. Neither is an easy place to grow wine, certainly compared to California. Oregon is about as marginal as Burgundy, well suited to Pinot Noir and aromatic whites, while Washington is warmer and drier—perhaps a producer of Cabernet Sauvignon in the Bordeaux mold, with rather more delicate fruit and keener acidity.

chile and argentina

Wine grapes arrived in Latin America with the Spanish missionaries, who used them for communion wine. And, frankly, this was the sort of wine that tasted so bad you needed a religious reason to drink it.

With over 300 days of sunshine a year, both countries would be too dry to make wine were it not for the Andes, which act as a giant dam, gathering snowfall all winter and releasing it as irrigating meltwater all summer.

Key regions
CHILE: MAIPO VALLEY, RAPEL VALLEY, CASABLANCA
ARGENTINA: MENDOZA

In Argentina, the vineyards make up for the relentless broiling sun by being planted at high altitude. There's no way you could get away with growing grapes in Europe at over 3,000 feet (900 meters), but in Argentina it's essential to counter the heat. Mendoza is the industry's headquarters, making fruit-packed reds. Tupungato, farther up into the chilly Andes, is gaining a reputation for pure, precise white wines, and some critics are keen on Torrontés, a lush, aromatic white that can work well with Asian food.

But (handily for a country that seems to survive on beef) Argentina is really about red wines. The damsony Malbecs, in particular, can be excellent, and since hardly anyone else in the world grows it, they represent a real point of difference.

In Chile it's a different story, with familiar grape varietals to the fore. The industry was founded by copper barons and industrialists in the 19th century.

Seeing themselves as aristocrats, they built châteaux and planted their wine estates with regal French grapes from Bordeaux and Burgundy. Cabernet and Chardonnay are still Chile's most-planted red and white grapes by some distance.

The best-known wine valleys are south of the capital, Santiago. Maipo produces elegant, minty Cabernet Sauvignons, while those from Rapel have a little more richness and weight. Indeed, the latter is the spiritual homeland of Chile's own grape oddity, Carmenère. This variety originated in France, but is incredibly tricky to grow and nowadays only really exists west of the Andes.

Syrah/Shiraz is growing enormously in popularity, and there are one or two good Pinot Noirs from the regions Leyda and Casablanca. The latter remains your best bet for Chilean white wines, with Sauvignon Blanc generally performing better than Chardonnay.

south africa

You might think that a country on the southern tip of Africa would be far too hot to make decent wine. And certainly the **flag-cracking sunshine** that beats down on the majestic beauty of the Cape throughout high summer is pretty intense.

But there are two big factors softening the climate at Africa's southern tip: the Atlantic and Indian oceans, which meet just east of Cape Town. The result is that, whether the wind comes from the southeast or the southwest, the Cape benefits from a **cooling sea breeze**.

Key regions
STELLENBOSCH, PAARL, FRANSCHHOEK, WALKER BAY, ELGIN, ROBERTSON

The industry began in the 17th century with Dutch settlers in Cape Town, but soon moved inland to the gorgeous fertility of Stellenbosch, whose multiple slopes and valleys offer great photography for the tourists and dozens of different options for sun and wind exposure to grape growers. The region's Cabernet Sauvignons can be of the highest class.

The wind has usually died out by the time it gets to Paarl, farther inland, and this hotter region (whose name means "pearl" in Afrikaans) is acquiring a reputation for heat-loving "Rhône varietals" like Syrah.

OK, so making decent red wines in this climate is understandable, but surely it's impossible to make good, fresh white wine? Oddly, no. Sure, a bottle of non-varietally labeled South African white wine is unlikely to linger long in the drinker's memory. But by planting vineyards on slopes that face away from the fierce mid-afternoon sun and growing either up on the hills (to catch the wind) or nearer to the coast (where it's cooler), places like Walker Bay, Robertson, Elgin, and Durbanville Hills are able to make some really excellent Chardonnays, Sauvignon Blancs, and Chenin Blancs.

In fact, the Cape is one of the most genuinely exciting areas in the wine world. The introversion generated in decades past by apartheid-induced isolation has been thrown off and, with dozens of small- to medium-sized wineries springing up every year, this is a country whose wine industry is brimming with energy and ideas.

australia

Australia has probably done more than any other country to **redraw the map** of the modern wine world. Not only do her wines fill shelves from Trondheim to Texas, but her winemakers have taken their knowledge and experience to just about everywhere that the vine is grown to help produce the stuff. An entire generation has grown up on well-priced, **well-fruited** Australian Cabernet Sauvignons, Shirazes, and Chardonnays that simply knock the competition into a cocked hat.

Key regions
McLAREN VALE, PADTHAWAY, CLARE VALLEY, LANGHORNE CREEK, BAROSSA VALLEY, YARRA VALLEY, HUNTER VALLEY, MARGARET RIVER

So what's the secret of their success? Well, first of all, they were quick to embrace new technology and drive new thinking, allowing them to make the most of what they had. Second, while there are vintage variations, Australia's climate is pretty reliable, making it relatively easy to make decent wine year after year.

A lot of Australia's cheaper wine comes from an area called the Riverland—an immense, flat, sun-drenched area where nothing would grow were it not for irrigation. On these huge plains, viticulture is large-scale, cheap, and easy; the wines, if not particularly complex, are at least reliably cheerful and fruity.

The Riverland is in South Australia, which is very definitely the headquarters of Australia's wine industry, scattering north, south, and east of the city of Adelaide. The most famous name in South Australia, for lovers of Cabernet Sauvignon at least, is probably Coonawarra, 200 miles southeast of the city. A remote, marshy place, it is neither big nor beautiful, but the Cabernet Sauvignons grown on the thin, rust-colored strip of "terra rossa" soil that runs through it are vibrant, focused, and long-lived—proof that France doesn't have a monopoly on terroir.

Coonawarra is relatively cool, but McLaren Vale, a low-lying area of gentle hills just south of Adelaide, bakes in the heat, producing lush, chocolatey Shiraz and cassis-laden Cabernet Sauvignon in the process.

The Barossa Valley, settled by Germans in the 1850s, also does good things with Shiraz and Cabernet. But both the Barossa and the Clare Valley manage to pull off the rare trick of making thumping warm-climate reds as well as super-elegant Rieslings higher up the valleys. In Clare, the latter are grown in the sort of slaty soil that would make a German winemaker homesick, and they are probably the best Rieslings that the New World can manage with the grape, though the cool Adelaide Hills, just east of the city, stake a fair claim, too.

Australia's best-known cool-climate area is the Yarra Valley, an hour or so's drive northeast of Melbourne.

It's an attractive, genteel sort of place (as you might expect from a region that was settled mostly by Swiss), and its cooler climate gives wines that are decidedly different from what most of us would consider typically Australian.

Yes, the fruit is fully ripe, but there's also a poise and elegance to the wines that can only come from grapes ripening slowly and gently and retaining some of their acidity. The latter characteristic, in fact, is the reason why Australia's quality sparkling wine production is based here.

If the Yarra is cool by Australian standards, then Tasmania, off the southeastern corner of Australia, is just plain cool. There's some very good sparkling wine made here, too, as well as some almost European Pinot Noirs and racy white wines. In this marginal climate, though, vintage variation is inevitably far more of an issue than in the rest of the country.

No such problems in Western Australia (WA), which basks in more or less nonstop sun for six months of the year. Indeed, the most northerly of the wine regions would be too hot to make wine anywhere nearly as good as they do, were it not for the winds (not breezes) that race in off the Indian Ocean.

Margaret River is the best-known area in WA, probably because it is farther south and therefore cooler. It's reckoned to have a climate similar to that of Bordeaux, but with less frost and, er, more kangaroos (which eat vine shoots, much to the chagrin of Australian winemakers), so it's no surprise that Margaret River's best wines are made with Bordeaux varietals like Cabernet Sauvignon, Merlot, Semillon, and Sauvignon, though there are also some good Shirazes. The wines are intense, ripe, flavorful, and sufficiently well structured to last for many years; for this reason, many now feel it is here, not Coonawarra, that is the best Cabernet-producing area in Australia.

However, arguably the biggest noise in Australian wine at the moment is being made in the Great Southern area southeast of Margaret River, where a series of exciting new cool- (or cooler-) climate regions is starting to make its mark. Mount Barker is famous for its Cabernet Sauvignon, Pemberton for Riesling and Chardonnay, while Frankland River is fast becoming the most-talked-about area for Shiraz in the whole country, with some of it even ending up in the country's most famous wine, Grange.

new zealand

New Zealand is different from the rest of the New World wine-producing countries. While the likes of South Africa, California, and Australia are mainly engaged in a battle to minimize the effects of the ferocious sun, New Zealand's growers fret about rain. The former's wines are reasonably consistent from one year to the next, while those from New Zealand can vary enormously in quality and (particularly) quantity from vintage to vintage.

Key regions
MARLBOROUGH, HAWKES BAY, CENTRAL OTAGO, MARTINBOROUGH

In some ways, then, New Zealand is the most European of the New World producers. And yet it is not through copying, but by practically reinventing, one of Europe's best-known grape varieties that the country made its mark.

Think New Zealand and most people think Sauvignon Blanc, specifically Sauvignon Blanc from Marlborough. This area at the top of the cooler South Island is just about ideal for the grape. There's plenty of sun but no searing heat, and just about no chance of rain before the grapes are picked. The result: a long, slow ripening period, absolutely perfect for capturing all those aromatic flavors in Sauvignon Blanc. And what flavors they are: grass, gooseberries, peppers, nectarines, peaches, mangoes, even blackcurrants. No wonder the world fell in love with Marlborough Sauvignon Blanc.

Other grape varieties are grown in Marlborough, but they don't perform anything like as reliably or, for the most part, as well as Sauvignon. But don't, whatever you do, make the mistake of thinking that New Zealand is all about one grape.

In the North Island, where it's warmer, there are some good, peachy Chardonnays with plenty of poise, while the South Island makes very good sparkling wine and increasingly attractive Rieslings and Pinot Gris. The latter "aromatic" varietals are only now starting to appear in any numbers—but already they have a good reputation.

Hawkes Bay, near the Art Deco town of Napier, two-thirds of the way down the east coast, is the best wine-growing area on the North Island. It gets huge amounts of sunshine (though not boiling heat) and can make high-quality Cabernet Sauvignons, Merlots and, increasingly, Shiraz, much of it grown on the Gimblett Gravels. "The Gravels" may not have the same poetic ring as Margaux, but this former riverbed has similar soils to one of Bordeaux's finest appellations, and is producing the sort of wines that make the world sit up and take notice.

The same goes for Central Otago in the South Island. Surrounded by spectacular mountains and lakes, Otago is decidedly cool and is proving itself to be arguably the best place for making the finest (as opposed to merely decent) expressions of Pinot Noir outside Burgundy, though Martinborough, near the capital, Wellington, runs it close.

grape varieties and WINE styles

From King Cabernet to unassuming Sémillon, a little knowledge of the different grape varieties can help you predict what the wine in your glass will taste like.

Cabernet Sauvignon is the world's most-planted quality red grape variety—the secret behind both some of the most expensive red wines in the world and a million bottles of cheap and cheerful plonk. Not all grapes are as at home on the president's table as they are in your kitchen: Cabernet is laudably democratic. Just about anyone who's ever drunk wine has tried it, and most people love it—it's that kind of grape.

cabernet sauvignon

Cabernet can deliver a good whack of blackcurrant flavor that stays on your tastebuds long after you've swallowed it. Its flavor palette also takes in other fruits like plums, black cherries, and damsons, plus non-fruit characteristics such as cedar, tobacco, dark chocolate, mint, and eucalyptus. Most Cabernet Sauvignon spends time aging in oak, so you're also likely to find vanilla or coconut wood aromas.

Cabernet needs a fair bit of sun to ripen—one of the reasons it does so well in New World countries. Pick before it's fully ripe, and you get thin, stingy fruit, and tannins that could strip the enamel from your teeth. Cabernet grapes, you see, are small and thick-skinned. Since grape skins are responsible for both color and tannin in a wine, and Cabernet has a high skin-to-pulp ratio, that means plenty of color and tannin. These are fine when allied to nice ripe fruit flavors, but if the grapes are picked before those flavors have developed you're left with not much taste, and lots of mouth-puckering tannin. (The tannins can be so fierce that the wines need years of aging before they are approachable.) To get real complexity in Cabernet, it needs to be planted where it can ripen fully, but slowly (so somewhere not too hot). The longer the flavors build up in the grape, the more character it will have, as well as sugar.

Cabernet Central is the stony, gravelly soils of Bordeaux, home to the most famous wine estates in the world. The five "first growth" wines in the Médoc are Châteaux Haut-Brion, Lafite, Latour, Margaux, and Mouton Rothschild. All five major in Cabernet.

Just about every Bordeaux red wine is a blend of at least two grape varietals. Australia, California, and the like might produce 100% Cabernet Sauvignons and

label them as such, but in Bordeaux, blending has always been king. Cabernet and Merlot, particularly, work very well together. Dark, brooding Cabernet gives structure to Merlot's soft, round, plumminess. Bergerac, to the west ("the poor man's Bordeaux"), has similar soils and microclimate to Bordeaux, and can also knock out a decent bottle of Cabernet. Here, it's frequently blended with Cabernet Franc.

In the States, Cabernet really put Napa on the map. With more sun and more reliable weather than in France, Californian winemakers can ripen Cabernet more easily, and suit their style to their climate. They leave the fruit on the vine to make sure tannins are super-ripe and the mouthfeel is soft and generous, with no hint of toughness or astringency. Although accessible young, the super-expensive top bottles can age for many years.

Being a grower in Chile is about as stress-free as it gets—the climate is perfect for Cabernet Sauvignon, and it is Chile's biggest varietal by some distance. Nearly all Chile's vines grow in the Central Valley, in regions such as Aconcagua Valley, Maipo, Rapel, Maule, and Bío-Bío.

Huge areas are given over to Cabernet in the hot, dry, Australian interior. In places like the Riverina, the burning sun ripens Cabernet year after year, giving wines with good color, alcohol, and flavor—but no real character. South Australia's best Cabernets are from Coonawarra; powerful, cassis-flavored wines with ripe tannins and leather, earth, and licorice elements, which age superbly. McLaren Vale gives similarly black-fruited wines (often with a brush of chocolate), and those of the Barossa Valley are big and bold. Margaret River's Cabernets (often "Bordeaux blends" with Merlot, Cabernet Franc, and so on) have admirers the world over for their elegance and finesse. The wines have a mulberry, blackberry leafiness and a full tannic finish, rather like those in Bordeaux. Even top wines in New World countries tend to be drinkable young.

South Australia's best Cabernets are from Coonawarra; powerful, cassis-flavored wines with ripe tannins and leather, earth, and licorice elements, which age superbly.

The best things often come in pairs. Think Fred Astaire and Ginger Rogers, think John Lennon and Paul McCartney; hell, more prosaically, why not think ham and eggs? Well, the wine world's equivalent of these famous duos is Merlot and Cabernet Sauvignon. The two are found together to great effect in the vast majority of reds from the world's most famous wine region, Bordeaux.

merlot

Most people know Bordeaux for its chunky Médoc Cabernets and grand châteaux, but in fact Merlot is the region's most-planted grape variety. And more New World winemakers are following suit, mixing the two grapes together to make a "Bordeaux blend" of their own—often called "meritage" in the U.S.

Look at Merlot's flavor profile and it's easy to see why it complements Cabernet Sauvignon so well—and why the cheaper Merlot is such a hit on its own. Cabernet is often called aristocratic, but Merlot is approachable. Its flavors are plummy or round and, with lower tannins, it's softer than Cabernet. Also, it ages more quickly, making it accessible younger.

Where sometimes you need to work hard to get a smile out of Cabernet, Merlot walks out of your glass and gives you a big grin. These differences in personality are the reason why the Bordelais often talk about a vintage being a "Cabernet year" or a "Merlot year." If it's hot enough to ripen Cabernet, the chances are it's too dry for Merlot; if it's cool and damp enough for Merlot, the Cabernets will probably be a bit on the skinny side. In fact, Merlot is often described as "filling out" Cabernet Sauvignon—adding a little roundness to the latter's tougher structure.

It's at its most pumped up in the super-rich (and super-expensive) wines of châteaux like Pétrus and Le Pin, from Pomerol, or Pavie, L'Evangile, and Angélus in St-Émilion. These are wines of great power and concentration, which can age beautifully for decades and need to be left for a long time before opening. But in this they're fairly atypical since, unlike the Cabernet-dominant wines from farther west, most right-bank wines—even pretty good ones—start to drink reasonably well after just a few years.

If you're tempted to go expensive with Merlot, look for wines from St-Émilion and Pomerol; the mid-ranking estates can be surprisingly good value.

Outside Bordeaux, Merlot's history is patchier. With the exception of Margaret River, way out west, Australia hasn't really got to grips with the grape yet, while New Zealand's versions veer from unmissable to undrinkable. There are a few good examples in South Africa and, particularly, the Americas, although Chile has discovered that a lot of its "Merlot" is actually another grape entirely (see below), and the country is having real problems with the genuine article. In California, the grape is widely planted, giving wines of softness and generosity, if no great excitement.

This is where Merlot's problems outside Bordeaux start. While it can pull off the "fleshy and approachable" routine extremely well, it hasn't really got the hang of "elegant." Those cool, clay soils and temperate climate that can make right-bank Bordeaux so special just aren't replicable anywhere else, and wineries often mistake alcoholic power for higher quality. If you buy a Merlot-based (or 100% Merlot) wine from the New World at the upper end of the price scale, you're likely to be left wondering where the extra money went. More fruit and more time in oak don't necessarily make for a better wine, and they certainly don't confer character.

So if you're tempted to go expensive with Merlot, look for wines from St-Émilion and Pomerol; only the very top wines are really expensive, and in fact, the mid-ranking estates can be surprisingly good value.

For most purists, a great Cabernet Sauvignon is better than a great Merlot, but while a bad Cabernet can be a painful experience Merlot nearly always manages to give you something worth drinking— it's that kind of willing-to-please grape variety.

CARMENÈRE—THE MERLOT THAT WASN'T

Outside Bordeaux and, to an extent, California, the country most associated with Merlot is Chile. But it turns out that many Chilean Merlot vines are actually another French grape varietal, Carmenère. How the Chileans mistook Carmenère for Merlot is a mystery, since it looks different and ripens weeks later. But there are similarities in its soft, sweet, dark-fruit flavor and easy tannins. And, like Merlot, it blends well with Cabernet Sauvignon; it's Friday-night wine.

shiraz

Say the name out loud, go on. Shiraz. As in Shiraz-matazz, as in "all that Shiraz." Well, it tastes like it sounds: exotic, jazzy, lively, hedonistic. No wonder it's the 21st century's answer to Cabernet Sauvignon and Chardonnay: the grape varietal that wineries want to grow and wine-lovers want to drink.

Actually, Shiraz has two names; it's known in Europe as Syrah (to rhyme with "mirror"). It's fitting, because this grape has something of a multiple personality, capable of making wine in a wide range of styles. Grow it somewhere relatively cool and it will give you pretty, red, raspberry fruits and distinctly spicy aromas. Stick it somewhere hot and you get full-on rich, dark blackberry flavors, overlaid with chocolate and plums. The Aussies, meanwhile, have used it to make fortified wines and even vivacious sparkling reds.

The beauty of Shiraz/Syrah is its tolerance. It doesn't have ragingly high tannins or acidity, and it gives of its fruit generously. You can make bad Shiraz, but it's much harder to get wrong than, say, Pinot Noir.

Shiraz, incidentally, is the name of a city in Iran. Popular mythology has it that the grape migrated, over many years, from the Middle East up to France, settling in the Rhône Valley, where it found the steep slopes around the mighty river very much to its liking. Now, in the same way that Bordeaux is the spiritual home of Cabernet Sauvignon and Merlot, and Burgundy of Pinot Noir and Chardonnay, so the Rhône is the heartland of what the French call Syrah.

The Rhône, of course, is a long river. A very long river, in fact. At its northern end, France feels, well... northern: cool, damp, and hilly, with winds so strong that the vines have to be staked to the hillside terraces. In the south, as it disgorges into the Mediterranean, the countryside is herb-scented and drier, the light more luminous, the pace of life slower.

And southern Rhône Syrah matches its geography, giving wines that are softer and rather more relaxed. Here it is usually one of a blend of grapes that can also include any (or all) of Grenache, Mourvèdre, Cinsaut, and Carignan, the wines typically warming and approachable but still powerful. Any combination of these grapes anywhere else in the world is often referred to as a "Rhône blend."

Syrah really comes into its own in the north, though. Here, with no other red grapes in sight, it becomes a center-stage soloist rather than a member of the orchestra. The vines perch on steep, granitic slopes that tumble down to the river and greedily absorb the sun. (Côte Rôtie, the appellation with the most expensive wines, means "roasted slope.") Hermitage, the other A-list area in the Rhône, is named after the small chapel near its summit and is one of France's very best wine-producing areas. Both these places give heady wines of power and perfume that can age for years. Cornas, St-Joseph, Crozes-Hermitage, and St-Péray are good, though less elegant, northern Rhône appellations.

For all France's pedigree, many argue that the grape is now doing its best work in Australia, where it's been planted for a long, long time and where it seems to like the hot, dry weather. The most famous

McLaren Vale Shirazes aren't exactly shy: rich, succulent, and stuffed with fruit, they're a meal in themselves.

examples come from the heat of the Barossa: big, hedonistic, chocolatey wines with head-spinning alcohol and a whack of spice. Those from McLaren Vale aren't exactly shy, either: rich, succulent, and stuffed with fruit, they're practically a meal in themselves. This big, extrovert style is what most people think of when you mention Aussie Shiraz, but cooler areas like Mount Barker in the far southwest or Victoria's wine regions make high-class Shiraz in a more restrained, peppery, almost European style.

South Africa, too, is starting to have some success with the Rhône's finest, sometimes as a single varietal and sometimes as a Rhône blend, while early Chilean examples (the grape was planted there in the late 1990s) show an appealingly soft succulence that augurs well for the future. The grape is still reasonably experimental in California, too, where the best examples (which can be very good) come from the Central Coast.

SHIRAZ AND VIOGNIER

Syrah is not blended with any other red grapes in the northern Rhône, but wineries sometimes add (quite legally) a small percentage of the white grape Viognier. Its luscious apricot and white-pepper flavors give a real lift to Syrah, if used in the right proportions. The Australians have picked this up, so we'll see more Shiraz/Viognier in years to come.

Was there ever a grape so exasperating as Pinot Noir? No other variety veers from the sublime to the ridiculous with such ease from one year to the next; even from one vineyard to the next in the same vintage. The free-thinker of the grape world, it is the hardest of all grapes to pin down, the hardest about which to generalize, and most definitely the hardest to tame.

pinot noir

The other "big" red grapes, Cabernet, Merlot, and Shiraz, are tolerant—at least to a degree—and will sometimes allow winemakers to cover up minor misjudgments or shortcomings in the weather to make something reasonable. But if the slightest thing goes wrong with Pinot Noir, whether in the vineyard or in the winery, boy, do you know about it! It's the sort of grape that would demand its own dressing room, 24 bunches of white lilies, chilled champagne, and a masseuse just to do a TV interview—then still wouldn't turn up.

Yet talk to winemakers all over the world and it is, practically without exception, the one grape variety that they most want to grow. Does that make them masochists? Well, yes and no. Everyone knows Pinot is hard work, but anyone who's ever drunk a really great Burgundy will understand why, for many

people, this is the grape varietal most capable of going beyond mere flavor and into a kind of sensual, liquid poetry that stays with you forever.

Oh, yes. Temperamental as an old diva it may be, but when the right mood takes Pinot Noir, the grape can truly deliver a sublime wine-drinking experience, offering wines of grace, elegance, and understated power that deliver a complexity so fine as to be almost weightless. Cherry, damson, and strawberry flavors are joined by a host of extraordinary savory aromas—of leather and leaf-mulch, of farmyards and bitter chocolate—all tied up with the silkiest of tannins.

Great Pinot isn't so much wine as art, a moment of beauty so effortless in its brilliance that you can't quite believe what you've just tasted. And it is the ability to deliver such jaw-dropping genius that

When the right mood takes Pinot Noir, the grape can truly deliver a sublime wine–drinking experience, offering wines of grace, elegance, and understated power.

affords the grape such indulgence. Winemakers will turn a blind eye to its tantrums in the hope and expectation that one year everything will go right for them and they will be able to capture that moment of sheer poetry that no other grape can manage.

So why is prissy Miss Pinot so hard to get right? The answer is that it only really expresses itself properly in fairly cool areas. Obviously, these cool-climate zones are, by their very nature, most prone to rain and clouds. And rain and clouds are high on the long list of things that Pinot Noir can't stand.

The grape's heartland is Burgundy; in fact, all red Burgundy (bar Beaujolais) is 100% Pinot Noir. The best wines come from the Côte de Nuits, a low ridge of hills that straggles north of Burgundy's HQ, the town of Beaune. The best estate is Domaine de la Romanée-Conti (or DRC, as it's known), but unless you're a millionaire, you'll probably never get to taste it. Production is tiny, and prices astronomical.

Fortunately, within the famous appellations like Vosne-Romanée, Echézeaux, Vougeot, Morey-St-Denis, and Gevrey-Chambertin, there are dozens of good vineyards and thousands of growers. That's the good news. The bad news is that a) they're still expensive, and b) because Pinot is so hypersensitive to its environment, and also so finicky to handle, it changes significantly in style, character, and quality from one appellation, vineyard, and grower to the next. It's what makes Burgundy so fascinating, but it's also what makes it so hellishly complicated.

Elsewhere in the world Pinot is, for the most part, less expressive at the top end, but rather more reliable and easier to understand. It's cheaper, too, though such things are, admittedly, relative for a grape that demands its pound of flesh and then some, both in the vineyard and the winery.

Probably the best New World examples come from New Zealand's cool South Island, in Marlborough and, especially, Central Otago, both of which get sun but no great heat, allowing the slow ripening that Pinot craves. Cooler areas of California, where the sea's influence is strong, like Russian River Valley, Carneros, and the Central Coast, are doing very good things with the grape, too, though there are plenty who prefer the more classical (and erratic) versions from farther north in Oregon, which is more naturally Burgundian in climate.

Cool, sea-affected Walker Bay in South Africa and Casablanca and Leyda in Chile are making good versions, while the drive for cooler sites in Australia is throwing up ever greater numbers there as well.

cabernet franc

It's tempting to think of Cabernet Franc as "the other Cabernet," a bit like a younger sibling, destined to be overshadowed by its famous big brother. Cab Franc (as it's usually abbreviated) doesn't have the power, presence, or longevity of Cabernet Sauvignon.

That doesn't make it inferior—just different. Like Cabernet Sauvignon, Cabernet Franc is planted in Bordeaux, but unlike its brother, it's usually found on the cooler clay soils of the right bank, with Merlot. Since it ripens earlier than Cabernet Sauvignon, it has more chance of being picked before the weather breaks, making it a safe bet for growers. But it's more than that. Its soft, red-fruit flavors are attractive, and in Bordeaux it often adds a herbaceous twist to the wines. Château Cheval Blanc, incidentally, one of the best of all Bordeaux, is predominantly Cab Franc.

Some of the grape's best wines are from the Loire, in Chinon, Bourgueil, and St-Nicolas-de-Bourgueil. Here it can give wines of no small charm, with a youthful raspberry and strawberry flavor that still ages for years. Of the three appellations, those from Chinon are usually the softest and silkiest, and can even be drunk chilled with meaty fish like monkfish.

Apart from large (mostly undistinguished) plantings in northeastern Italy, and the occasional flash of inspiration from producers in the New World, Cab Franc hasn't shown much talent outside its homeland.

sangiovese

Sangiovese is planted **all over Italy**, and if you've ever drunk Italian wine, you've probably had some. You just wouldn't know it, because Italians don't usually **name** the **grape variety** on the bottle.

You may have heard of the wine style in which this grape is the main component: Chianti. Chianti used to be a byword for thin, acidic, nasty wines from Tuscany, but now the grape is showing what it is capable of: fantastic, mid-weight, cherry-and-plum-flavored wines with good acidity and tannin. These aren't wines to drink on their own, but their easy weight and good structure make them fabulous with food.

For most wine lovers, Sangiovese reaches its pinnacle when it is mixed with Cabernet Sauvignon, which adds weight, silkiness, more depth, and ageability. These so-called Supertuscans are among the classiest, most expensive wines in the world. The grape isn't widely planted outside Italy, but some producers elsewhere (especially in California) are making good wine with it.

grape varieties and wine styles

zinfandel

Zappy name, *zappy* kind of grape. Zin has been around in California since the 19th century and when it's treated properly can make some of **America's best** and most **individual** wines.

Genetically, Zinfandel has been traced back to a southern Italian grape called Primitivo, which must have made its way to the New World in the pockets of some far-sighted immigrant. But in California it has taken on a life of its own, giving big, rich, spicy wines of depth and character. It's tolerant, too, and is able to give you a fulfilling glassful both from cooler areas of Sonoma and the hot Central Valley—though the wines are very different in character.

White Zinfandel is the name given to an easy-drinking, sweetish blush (pink) version, made from the same grape. It's OK when drunk chilled, but not very exciting.

This is the **cornerstone** of one of the world's absolutely classic wine styles: Spanish **Rioja**. You wouldn't know it from **looking** at the bottle, though, because very few labels tell you that.

tempranillo

Tempranillo is an easygoing, early-ripening grape (*temprano* is Spanish for "early"—hence the name), which usually means it's safely harvested and in the winery before the worst of the autumn weather arrives. It's planted (under a variety of different regional names) right across Spain.

Generally speaking, Tempranillo gives a ripe, round, generous dollop of red-fruit flavors (strawberries and plums are common), developing more complexity once it's had a bit of time in oak barrels. Open and accessible, this is a wine that drinks well young, so (barring top Riberas and Riojas) don't keep it too long.

If Hollywood was ever going to make a film of a grape variety's life story, they would probably choose Malbec. The story begins in the rustic open spaces of southwestern France, where our hero is busy being used in small amounts, blended with other grapes, right across the region.

malbec

His is a supporting role, but he knows he can do better and hops on a boat to South America, where he settles in the vineyards of Argentina. The locals love him, pamper him, and give him top billing, and before long he's a star, drunk by presidents and peasants alike and shipped all over the world, with his name in big letters on the bottle. In Argentina, Malbec is sultry, perfumed, and silky. In Chile, it can be even darker and more brooding still, with definite licorice flavors.

grenache

Grenache is one of the key grapes in probably the most densely planted area of vineyards in the world, across the south of France and into northern Spain. So why, you may wonder, isn't it a household name? The answer's simple. These areas historically made their wines with a blend of different grape varieties and didn't list them all on the label.

So if you've ever drunk a southern French red (or a Côtes du Rhône), you've probably drunk a wine with a fair bit of Grenache in it. If you've had a glass of Châteauneuf-du-Pape, that's just about all Grenache.

The role of Grenache in blended wines is usually one of providing alcohol, which it does very well. But when it's on its own or allowed to dominate (as in the big, butch monsters from Châteauneuf-du-Pape), you can savor its cheerful red-fruit and spice flavors. Done well, Grenache is as warming as a log fire.

It hasn't really caught on in the New World for quality wines yet. The Aussies and Californians use it to make fortified or cheap jug wine, but this is changing. You may not see it much on its own, but it's ever more likely to form the "G" part of a GSM compound—Grenache, Shiraz, Mourvèdre.

There are a few **oddball** producers around the world who occasionally plonk an **experimental** bottle of Gamay on the table at the end of a tasting, but really this grape is all about one place, and one place only: Beaujolais.

gamay

Bog-standard Beaujolais is light, soft, fruity, and fairly unmemorable. It works OK as a glass of undemanding glug, and can be attractive chilled with barbecued food or fish. Challenging it isn't, though it scores fairly well in the drinkability stakes as long as you don't expect something big and chewy.

Beaujolais Villages wines have rather more concentration than straight Appellation Contrôlée Beaujolais and, frankly, are a better bet. The best examples combine attractive soft, strawberry fruit with fresh acidity and beguiling, wispy tannins. But if you want something really interesting, look for wines from one of Beaujolais' ten crus—the top growing areas in the region.

They're all made from the same Gamay grape, and grown no more than eight miles apart, yet their characters are very different. From the dark, brooding, almost metallic wines from Morgon and Moulin-à-Vent to the cheery fruit of Chiroubles and Fleurie, these are the different faces of Gamay reflected through each appellation's terroir. This makes Beaujolais an interesting theme for a wine tasting (see pages 218–223).

Pinotage is a divisive grape variety. A bit like modern jazz, you either love it or hate it. Just about all of it is grown in South Africa, where it was created in the 1920s by a professor who wanted to make a grape that had both pedigree and toughness.

pinotage

He crossed Pinot Noir with Cinsaut, and the wine world has been arguing about it ever since. Much of the controversy stemmed from the indifferent wines that the South Africans were making with it as recently as 10 years ago. But this seems to have been more of a problem with winemakers not knowing how to vinify it properly (it's a new grape, remember) rather than an inherent problem with the varietal itself, and 21st-century versions are way better.

There are two main styles. Cheaper wines tend to be light, juicy, and raspberry-flavored, while the more premium examples can have attractive swirling, spicy dark fruit and deserve to be taken seriously. "Cape blends" (a mix of Bordeaux varieties like Cabernet and Merlot with Pinotage) are growing in popularity in the Cape and fetch increasingly high prices.

famous red wines

Cabernet Sauvignon

regions The Médoc villages in Bordeaux: Margaux, St-Estèphe, Pauillac, St-Julien; Napa Valley and Alexander Valley (California); Maipo and Colchagua Valleys (Chile); Stellenbosch (South Africa); Coonawarra and Margaret River (Australia)

producers Châteaux Lafite, Latour, Mouton Rothschild, Margaux, Haut-Brion, Cos d'Estournel, Pichon-Longueville, and Lynch-Bages (all Bordeaux's left bank); Screaming Eagle, Opus One, Harlan Estate (California); Almaviva (Chile)

Merlot

regions Pomerol and St-Émilion (Bordeaux's right bank); Rapel Valley (Chile); Napa Valley and Sonoma Valley (California)

producers Famous Merlot-dominant estates in Bordeaux include Châteaux Pétrus, Pavie, Trotanoy, Lafleur, and l'Angélus

Syrah/Shiraz

regions Côte Rôtie, Hermitage, St-Joseph, Crozes-Hermitage, Cornas (all northern Rhône); Barossa Valley, McLaren Vale (Australia)

producers Chapoutier, Chaves, Jaboulet, Guigal (all northern Rhône); Penfolds Grange, Henschke Hill of Grace (Australia); Montes Folly (Chile)

Pinot Noir

regions Gevrey-Chambertin, Vosne-Romanée, Vougeot, Morey-St-Denis, Chambolle-Musigny, Nuits-St-Georges (Burgundy); Russian River Valley and Carneros (California); Marlborough and Central Otago (New Zealand)

producers Domaine de la Romanée-Conti, Bonneau du Martray, Henri Jayer, Louis Jadot (all Burgundy); Felton Road (Central Otago)

Sangiovese

regions Chianti and Montalcino (Italy)

producers Villa Cafaggio, Antinori (Chianti); Biondi-Santi (Montalcino)

Zinfandel

regions Mendocino and Lodi (California)

producers Ravenswood, Ridge

Tempranillo

regions Rioja and Ribera del Duero (Spain)

producers Marques de Riscal and Muga (Rioja); Pesquera de Duero (Ribera del Duero)

Malbec

region Mendoza (Argentina)

producer Catena

Grenache

region Châteauneuf-du-Pape (southern Rhône)

producers Domaines Perrin and Henri Bonneau

From the shores of the Great Lakes to the Cape of Good Hope, Chardonnay is a grape that travels with a smile. And if it turns up its roots in disgust at a location, then it's probably a site that isn't fit for growing anything. Of all the top grape varieties, Chardonnay is probably the easiest to grow. Give it some sun and a bit of water, and it will turn out juicily ripe grapes, even if a location's really too hot or too cold.

chardonnay

In the vineyard the only two major worries with Chardonnay are that its early budding makes it vulnerable to spring frosts, while if there's too much rain and the grapes swell, its thin skins can split. Another problem is, as you might expect for such a positive grape, that left to its own devices the vine will churn out stacks of grapes and bushy canopies of leaves—neither of which improves quality.

Conscientious growers work hard at limiting the vine's productivity, but less scrupulous producers, in search of quantity rather than quality, often choose Chardonnay. For high yields of unremarkable but drinkable plonk, there's no better grape.

Some in the wine world worry about its ubiquity, but it's hard to give much credence to the ABC (Anything But Chardonnay) brigade, because Chardonnay is rarely actually bad. Characterless, yes, but still highly drinkable, which is why Chardonnay is so appealing to consumers. The grape delivers at any price, with a consistency and flexibility that put every other grape variety—red or white—to shame.

So, what does Chardonnay actually taste like? One of the more neutral-flavored grapes, Chardonnay is often characterized by a soft melony aroma. This offers a clean slate on which both the place where it's grown and the winemaker can leave their marks; the finished wine's flavors can go from apples, melons, and lemons to extraordinarily intense aromas of nuts, mangoes, quince, honeysuckle, figs, and honey.

This clean slate can mean highly drinkable wine from unexciting raw material. On the other hand, it can mean wines that have been molded to fit an internationally acceptable profile, rather than being allowed to express their site's character. The use (or

not) of wood is arguably the most important element. Unlike most white grapes, Chardonnay loves oak, which gives it a spicy, toasty, vanilla flavor that gives a real mouth-filler in your glass.

Add too much wood, though, and you get a wine where oak dominates and all freshness is lost. This was common in the early 1990s, especially in Australian and California Chardonnays, some of which practically had to be cut with a saw before drinking.

Burgundy is Chardonnay's homeland, the place that gives the most complex and inspiring expressions of the grape anywhere in the world. Chablis, 125 miles (200 km) south of Paris, is Burgundy's most northerly outpost. The name might have been appropriated in some countries for generic dry whites that have nothing to do with Chardonnay, but this small, chilly region makes thrilling wines when it gets it right. The best wines from the best vineyards (Grands Crus) are toned and stony, with flashes of citrus fruit and flowers. They can (and sometimes need to) be aged for at least 10 years, though standard Chablis and Petit Chablis wines are best drunk young. Chardonnay is also a key ingredient in champagne (see pages 116–120).

South of Chablis is Burgundy's heartland, the Côte d'Or. Farther south in the Côte Chalonnaise and the Mâconnais there's less of the limestone Chardonnay loves, resulting in soft, "Burgundy-lite" flavors.

For thousands of American wine lovers, white wine is Chardonnay. They like their whites big, round, and soft, with not too much acidity (which can constrain adventurous winemakers). Carneros, at the southern

The best wines from the best vineyards (Grands Crus) are toned and stony, with flashes of citrus fruit and flowers.

end of California's Napa Valley, and Sonoma County, are cool enough to produce good Chardonnay. Farther south, San Luis Obispo and the Santa Maria Valley are good areas, as is Chile's Casablanca Valley.

Aussie Chardonnay is the white-wine success story of the last 20 years. The Australians make lean, elegant wines from even hot, big-volume regions like the Riverland, where there's so much sun that the chance of grapes ripening too fast is a real problem. These wines, with pure, balanced fruit flavors, offer astonishing value for money: they're not exciting, but they're very gluggable. Best areas are the Adelaide Hills, the Yarra Valley, and Margaret River.

South Africa's Cape Province is also cool enough for Chardonnay; those from Elgin can be elegantly citrus, with lemon and even grapefruit flavors. In Walker Bay, you'll find wines with a finesse that can border on the Burgundian. Also worth watching is the Robertson area, which has limestone-rich soils.

Some top wines from the New World benefit from five to ten years in bottle, but the majority of Chardonnays won't improve significantly with time.

Indisputably the world's other "Big White," Sauvignon Blanc could hardly be more different in character from its buddy Chardonnay. While the latter is all soft mouth-feel and fruity aromas, Sauvignon (as it's usually called in the trade) is all perfume and zip. It's a lively sprite of a variety that delivers intense, aromatic flavors to your mouth in a big hit and then disappears, leaving your palate tingling.

sauvignon blanc

If Sauvignon Blanc were a perfume, it would be all top notes, which is one of the reasons it is such a good match with lighter food such as fish but tends to be swamped by white meats. If you're serving, say, chicken in a creamy sauce, you will probably want to leave the Sauvignon Blanc in the fridge.

Its homeland is France's Loire Valley, a beautiful area dotted with imposing 17th-century châteaux, where it makes fresh, rather beautiful wines. Sauvignon de Touraine—one of France's great bargain whites—typically tastes of juicy limes, cut grass, and blackcurrant leaves, and it's hard to think of anything more refreshing on a hot day. It's eminently drinkable, with cool acidity balanced by juicy fruit.

On the limestone hill of Sancerre, however, the wines take on a different character. Good examples are all flint, gunsmoke, and minerals, rather than fruit; intense, complex, austere whites that are arguably the finest seafood wines in the world, and can be priced accordingly. Unfortunately, the word "Sancerre" on the bottle doesn't guarantee quality. Standards vary alarmingly from producer to producer, so unless you've been given a recommendation or you know what you're looking for, think twice before shelling out extra cash. Certainly, if you like your whites upfront and fruity, you're not likely to be a fan of the region, however famous it might be. The critics and cognoscenti might love it, but Sancerre, very definitely, is an acquired taste.

The Sauvignon Blancs of Bordeaux, however, are far more approachable. Farther south than the Loire, the grapes tend to get rather more heat and sun, and

Sauvignon de Touraine typically tastes of juicy limes, cut grass, and blackcurrant leaves, and it's hard to think of anything more refreshing on a hot day.

the result is wines with a little more roundness and generosity—particularly since they're usually plumped up by being blended with Sémillon. White Bordeaux is one of the most appealing white wine styles in the world. It's always been overshadowed by the big-budget red wines that surround it, but it's a solid, reliable jobbing actor who turns in good performance after good performance while the Hollywood star steals all the headlines. The best white Bordeaux, from the Pessac-Léognan appellation, are high-quality, minerally wines that can age for many years.

Bordeaux and the Loire may be where Sauvignon Blanc was born and brought up, but for many people the grape has come to be associated with a country on the other side of the world: New Zealand. The region of Marlborough, at the top of the country's North Island, has made the grape its own in less than 20 years. The first grapes only went in there in 1975, but its reputation is already long established. The key to Marlborough's success with Sauvignon is that it gets lots of sun, but not excessive heat, and (usually) a super-long growing season. Put this all together and you get fully ripe grapes with lots of flavor complexity and plenty of the fresh acidity that's Sauvignon Blanc's trademark.

Not everyone likes the distinctive flavors of gooseberry, nectarines, passion fruit, and green pepper that fly out of the glass at you, but they make one of the few wines that is a decent match with Asian food, and they drink well on their own, too.

The grape hasn't really been a big player in Australia, which has always tended to prefer

Chardonnay, but in cooler areas, like Tasmania and the Adelaide Hills, it's starting to take off. The same goes for Chile. Ten years ago Sauvignon was definitely secondary to Chardonnay, but most winemakers now admit that their Sauvignon Blancs are the country's best white grape variety. The most superior by far are the luscious, tropical-fruited examples from the Casablanca Valley; many of those from elsewhere are at least partly made from the utterly inferior Sauvignon Blanc clone, Sauvignonasse.

South Africa has also taken to the grape, and like Chile, its Sauvignons tend to be more reliably good than its Chardonnays. Best areas are Walker Bay, Elgin, Durbanville, and cooler areas of Stellenbosch.

In the United States, Sauvignon Blanc remains very much in Chardonnay's shadow. It's sometimes barrel-fermented to give a richer, creamier wine style, called Fumé Blanc, which is less aromatic but has a bit more weight in the mouth.

Part of the trouble with Riesling is that it doesn't sound sexy. "Chardonnay" and "Sauvignon Blanc" have those wonderful soft French vowel sounds that positively demand to be rolled around the mouth, while "Riesling" is rather Germanic and spiky. And yet it is, probably, the most glorious white grape variety of them all. A hundred years ago, Rieslings from the top German estates were the most expensive wines (not just whites) in the world.

riesling

People prized them for their ability to age for decades and unparalleled complexity. Nowadays, though production is a large lake compared to the oceans of Sauvignon Blanc and Chardonnay slopping around the world, Riesling is (happily) gaining popularity again.

It doesn't travel with quite the same gay abandon as Chardonnay, which is one reason the New World countries have been slower to get the hang of it. Making decent Riesling is all about finding the right place—and that takes time. Europe's had thousands of years to get it right, so it would be unrealistic to expect the likes of New Zealand and South Africa to hit the bullseye in a few decades, especially because Riesling is, well, tricky. It likes things to be dry, but isn't a sun-worshipper, preferring the weather to be sunny well into the autumn rather than boiling hot over the summer. The trouble with this is that cool

places also tend to be rainy places, and while you can save Chardonnay, for instance, in a damp year, washed-out Riesling really isn't a great experience.

Hang on, you might be saying. Haven't I read something like this before? The answer is yes, about Pinot Noir. And, while Riesling can't match Pinot for sheer bloody-minded awkwardness, it is the most temperamental of the great white varieties. Grow it somewhere it likes, and do the right things, and it will reward you with a wine of rare depth and character. Plant it somewhere less suitable and you're in trouble.

For starters, Riesling is a naturally vigorous grape variety, so if your soil is too fertile, it will run wild, churning out zillions of grapes that haven't a chance of all getting ripe. And one thing you don't want to drink is under-ripe Riesling. Put it somewhere hot? You'll get grapes with plenty of sugar-ripeness, but

not a lot of flavor. Riesling's spritzy aromas can be burned out by too much sun, so there's no point growing it anywhere too steamy.

One of Riesling's defining characteristics is its acidity, which is high, high, high. In a well-made wine, this is definitely a Good Thing, since it allows the wine to age for decades while retaining its freshness, moving from peach and lime flavors to dried fruits and, sometimes, an amazing oiliness quite unlike any other grape. It gives even young wines a palate-zapping freshness that can leave you feeling that your mouth has just been hit with a high-pressure hose. Unfortunately, in years when rain or clouds stop the fruit from ripening well, you can end up with the unlovely combination of high acidity and low fruit. Bad Riesling is joyless, hard work.

It's to avoid such toughness that many German Rieslings are off-dry. A little natural sugar left in the wine after fermentation rounds out Riesling's flavors and helps to take the edge off the acidity. Balancing this fruit/sweetness/acidity triangle is what being a winemaker in Germany's premium Riesling regions of the Mosel and the Rheingau is all about. The best of these wines are a miracle of balance, with softly generous flavors and a whistle-clean finish. They're fantastic to drink on their own; because of their lower alcohol, they're good at lunch times; and they can also work well with spicy Asian or fusion food.

New World Rieslings, by contrast, are mostly dry. With more sun and heat than their German counterparts, the wines are plumper and fruitier, so there's no need to leave in any comforting sugar. The wines don't have the same taut elegance as European versions, but they are accessible and refreshing, and more flexible with food: a good match with fish, seafood, and creamy pork and chicken dishes. The best are from New Zealand and the Barossa and Clare valleys and Adelaide Hills in Australia.

grape varieties and wine styles

Grapes are like people. Some like to seek the limelight, noisily taking center stage whenever they can; others prefer to bump along in the background. Some like to see their name in lights, others are happy with a quiet mention every now and then. Some outperform their innate talent, while others remain brilliant but undiscovered. Now, guess which group Sémillon falls into…

sémillon

If Chardonnay is the sort of attention-seeking grape that blows air kisses at Oscar ceremonies, then Sémillon is the variety that slinks into the theater untroubled by photographers' flashbulbs. So unassuming is it, in fact, that there's a fair chance you've never heard of it, let alone knowingly drunk it. Yet the grape is a key player in two of the world's best-known and certainly best-loved wine styles, and once you've tuned into how darn good it can be, you'll wonder why it doesn't have a higher profile.

So, you think you've never drunk it? Well, if you've ever had a white Bordeaux, you've almost certainly drunk some Sémillon, since the region's whites are nearly always a blend of the latter and Sauvignon Blanc. The same goes for the lush dessert wines from Sauternes and Barsac, probably the world's best-known sweet wines (see pages 122–125 for more).

The Sauvignon/Sémillon joint venture is a good combination. If Sauvignon is all bones and energy, Sémillon is fatter, rounder, and more comfortable, adding lovely rich, honeyed tones to Sauvignon's peppy aromatics. It's that classic partnership of the mercurial motormouth and the silent giant who's slow to anger—and, like all classic partnerships, it works. The majority of Bordeaux's dry whites are from the Entre-Deux-Mers region, though the very best Sémillon/Sauvignons are from Pessac-Léognan, where the combination of low yields, gravelly soil, and oak fermentation gives wines of real attitude, complexity, and ageability.

Sémillon, in other words, can make not just cheerful quaffing wine but also some really high-quality offerings. So why the low profile? Well, it's partly because there aren't that many really good

With its lush honey, lime, and butterscotch characters, Sémillon is a very easy grape to get to like. If you've never tried it, you really should.

white Bordeaux compared to top-class reds, and partly because, this being France, the grape's name doesn't appear on the wine label, which explains why Sémillon's talents have been, if not undiscovered, then certainly under-appreciated for so long. The New World, of course, isn't so shy about putting the grape varietal at the forefront (how do you think Chardonnay, Merlot, Cabernet Sauvignon, et al, became the global phenomena that they are?), but alas, when it comes to white wines, most of them have followed the Chardonnay route, and few have done much with Sémillon.

The exception to this is, oddly, the king of New World Chardonnay, Australia, which has had sizeable plantings of Semillon (they drop the accent on the "e" Down Under) for well over a hundred years. The grape is grown with success from coast to coast. It makes some of the best (and most unusual) white wines from the quixotic Hunter Valley, north of Sydney; amazing, rich versions in the sun-baked Barossa Valley; and beautiful tropical-fruit-

flavored examples from the rather cooler vineyards of Margaret River, in the far west. Sometimes it is blended with Chardonnay to give big, lush wines, other times with Sauvignon Blanc à la Bordelaise, and sometimes stands as a single varietal.

While there are isolated examples of Sémillon produced from Africa to the Americas, no other country has the same kind of concentration of it

that either Bordeaux or Australia has, and few have tried to hammer home its point of difference. All of this is decidedly odd because, with its lush honey, lime, and butterscotch characters, Sémillon is a very easy grape to get to like. If you've never tried it, you really should. It's a good substitute for Chardonnay and can be drunk happily both on its own and with food.

Poor Chenin Blanc. It's planted in huge numbers all over the world, yet is very rarely talked about. Why? Because, to put it bluntly, most of the wine this grape makes is rubbish.

chenin blanc

Not that this is the fault of the grape itself, oh, no. In its purest form, Chenin Blanc can make some of the most intriguing wines in the world. Try a Vouvray or a Savennières from the central Loire Valley in France, and you'll find something that is intriguing, challenging, and often amazing value for money.

But in the past, in places like the U.S. and South Africa, the grape has been used as a workhorse to give lots of juice for cheap wine or brandy. Happily this is changing, and more good examples are emerging from these countries, especially South Africa, whose versions are juicily tropical.

Gewürztraminer is a mouthful in every sense of the word. Once memorably described by a thirsty customer at a winery in Australia as "Gee-whizz tram-driver," no wonder it's usually shortened to Gewürz (pronounced "Ga-vurts").

gewürztraminer

The name (which means "spicy Traminer") might be German, and the grape might be found there, but its heartland is Alsace, at France's eastern edge on the border with Germany. It makes powerfully aromatic wines, whose flavors don't so much float out of the glass as hang above it in a dense, perfumed cloud: lychees, roses, and Turkish delight are typical and make Gewürztraminer the most recognizable grape varietal in the world. Its big flavors make it a good wine to sip on its own, but it's also your best bet to accompany heavily flavored Chinese or Thai food.

Is red the new black? Is Monday the new Friday? And could Viognier be **the new Chardonnay?** Certainly, it's a grape that's becoming more and more fashionable, following its **small-town** beginnings in France's northern Rhône Valley.

viognier

Now the little country girl has traveled all over the world and is starting to attract the attention of the wine industry's bigwigs, who think that she might just have star potential.

When she learns her lines and puts her heart into the performance, Viognier gives rich, heady, apricot-flavored wines that are to die for. But give her a bad script in an unprepossessing location and her performances are wooden and flat, with little flavor. Still, there are ever more good examples coming from places as far apart as the south of France, California, Chile, and New Zealand. These wines tend to be soft, fun, and accessible, with gentle acidity—good Friday-night or takeout wines. But only in the Rhône's Condrieu does it attain true greatness.

Pinot Gris is something of a shadowy character, a **chameleon** grape that has a variety of identities depending on where it happens to be. Probably its best-known incarnation is Italian; as **Pinot Grigio,** it has propped up wine-bar lists all over the world.

pinot gris

Light, spritzy, and inoffensive (and capable of excellence when grown in the Alto Adige), it is an aperitif classic.

Head into France, specifically Alsace, and it's a different story. The grape has a different name (look for Tokay Pinot Gris) and character. Forget light and bouncy; the wines are rich and full-bodied with an utterly beguiling honeyed, briary smokiness. Acidity levels are low, and alcohol and mouthfeel levels fairly high, making this a wine that works with big white-meat dishes and spicy food—even with darker meat.

How so? Pinot Gris, a white grape, is actually a mutation of the red Pinot Noir. Many of the Alsace wines have the sort of light red-fruit flavors more associated with red wines than white. For many people, Alsace Pinot Gris is the gold standard for the grape.

In Germany, Grauburgunder (as it's known) can be a fun, fleshy concoction, while New Zealand and the U.S. (where it goes by its proper name) show encouraging signs of wines with appealing fruit and acidity.

Most grapes make wines that taste of fruit. Melons, pears, currants, strawberries: take your pick. Muscat is the only one that makes wine that actually tastes of grapes. It's a joyous, perfumed, aromatic character, and is sometimes used to give a little lift to otherwise dull wine.

muscat

Muscat's big downfall, though, is its structure—or lack of it. With very little acidity, it makes wines that are initially appealing, but rather flabby for table wine, and most of it goes to make either sparkling or fortified wine.

Italian Moscato d'Asti (light, fun, bouncy—good party wine) is an example of the former, while the French Muscat de Beaumes-de-Venise from the southern Rhône is one of the most widely available examples of the latter. Other great sweet wines are made in Australia, though, particularly in Victoria, and these Orange or Black Muscats can be good-value, heady dessert wines.

Marsanne is the Rhône's most impressive white grape, making powerful, distinctive wines with flavors of apples, pears, spice, and almonds. It's a high-alcohol wine with lowish acidity, but it blends well with its Rhône buddy, Roussanne, to make wines of depth and longevity.

marsanne

The most famous appellations for white Rhône are Crozes-Hermitage, St-Joseph, and, particularly, Hermitage, where it makes up just under a quarter of all the vines planted.

Alas, for those of an impatient bent, wines from this famous hill need to mature for up to a decade before showing off their flavors, which partly explains why the grape isn't more widely planted. The flavors might be intense and beguiling, but few people can be bothered to wait for them to reveal themselves. Having said that, the few New World examples (mostly from Australia, with a few hardy Californians) drink reasonably well when younger.

grape varieties and wine styles

famous white wines

Chardonnay
regions Puligny-Montrachet, Chassagne-Montrachet, Meursault, Chablis (Burgundy); Russian River Valley, Sonoma Coast, Santa Maria Valley (California); Adelaide Hills, Yarra Valley, Margaret River, Padthaway (Australia)
producers Henri Jayer, Comtes Lafon, Coche-Dury, Domaine de la Romanée-Conti (Burgundy); Laroche, Raveneau (Chablis); Chain of Ponds, Nepenthe, Cape Mentelle, Yattarna (Australia)

Sauvignon Blanc
regions Bordeaux, Sancerre, Pouilly-Fumé (France); Marlborough (New Zealand)
producers Henri Bourgeois, Pascal Jolivet (Sancerre); Didier Dagueneau (Pouilly-Fumé); Château la Louvière, Domaine de Chevalier (Bordeaux); Cloudy Bay, Villa Maria (New Zealand); Springfield, Iona (South Africa)

Riesling
regions Mosel, Rheingau, Pfalz (Germany); Clare Valley (Australia)
producers Müller-Catoir, Dr. Loosen, JJ Prüm (Germany); Petaluma, Jeffrey Grosset (Australia)

Gewürztraminer
region Alsace (France)
producers Trimbach, Zind-Humbrecht, Schoffit, Hugel

Sémillon

regions Bordeaux, Sauternes, Barsac (France); Hunter Valley (Australia)
producers Château d'Yquem, Château Suduiraut, Château Climens (Sauternes)

Chenin Blanc

regions Saumur, Savennières, Vouvray (Loire); Stellenbosch (South Africa)
producers Marc Brédif, Domaine Huet (Vouvray)

Viognier

region Condrieu (Rhône Valley)
producer Château Grillet

grape varieties and wine styles

Want to know what the hottest wine style is just now? It's rosé. Consumers all over the world are starting to tune in to how entertainingly gluggable it can be, and wineries from Australia to the Americas are adding pinks to their portfolios faster than you can say "serve chilled." Frankly, rosé deserves its renaissance.

rosé wines

For decades the only representation that the drink had on wine shelves all over the world was either something cheap, light, and not terribly exciting from the south of France, or bubblegum-flavored sugar-water. There's nothing inherently wrong with either of these styles—certainly, the latter did a good job of introducing lots of people to wine who otherwise wouldn't have gone near it—but they've tended to dominate the entire category and stopped other, more modern styles of rosé from gaining a foothold. While red and white wines have unquestionably moved on in the way they are made and packaged over the last 20 years, rosé remained resolutely—and puzzlingly—stuck where it was.

Well, no more. Rosés are being made modern and fruity, dry and trendy-looking; the sort of wines you want to show off, rather than hide, when guests come over. They're also being made from pretty much every red grape varietal you care to mention, with Syrah/Shiraz becoming especially popular.

How is rosé made? Well, first things first: let's scotch the idea that it's simply a blend of red and white wine. Some places do mix red and white to make pink, but in Europe this isn't permitted (with the notable exception of champagne). No, most rosé wine—and all the good stuff—is made from red grapes. To understand how you get rosé wine and not red from, say, your Cabernet Sauvignon, you need to understand how the color gets into red wines in the first place.

Squeeze a red grape and the juice will be the same color as a white grape's. But crush them and leave them in two separate pots for a while, stirring them occasionally, and you'll see a difference: the white juice will remain white and the red grape juice will have turned red. Why? Because color leaches out of the red grape skins and dyes the juice.

So, when making rosé, it's all about leaving the crushed grapes in contact with the juice for just the right amount of time to color it pink, which usually means a couple of days (rather than a week or more for reds), then siphoning off the liquid and vinifying it like a white wine. Since rosés are all about freshness of flavor, very few spend any time in oak.

In fact, the attraction of modern rosés at least is that they have plenty of good, zippy red-fruit character, but no tannin and, usually, a refreshing hit of palate-cleansing acidity, all of which makes them absolutely ideal for warm weather—especially barbecues. But they're also a good, enjoyable glugger for nights on the sofa, or a compromise on nights when one of you wants red and the other white.

The most famous rosé region in France is probably Anjou in the Loire, which makes gallons of the stuff, most of it no better than mediocre. Provence, too,

churns out lakes of pink wine, most of it of no great distinction either. The most expensive rosés in France (and probably the world) come from Tavel, in the southern Rhône. Gutsy and alcoholic, unlike just about any other rosé, they can age for a few years quite happily, although most wine-drinkers would probably prefer the Merlot-based examples from Bordeaux, which can be utterly charming.

Outside France, Spain makes a lot of *rosado*, and the Grenache-based offerings from Navarra (next to Rioja) are soft, round, and refreshing at any time of year, not just in summer.

In the New World, rosé was an endangered species a few years ago, but now, frankly, you can take your pick, since everyone's at it from New Zealand to Chile. White Zinfandel (a sweet blush wine from California) is one of the biggest rosé styles in the world and has been around for a while, but there are good, dry examples from the Golden State and beyond that pose less of a risk to your tooth enamel and still have plenty of fruit flavor.

Modern rosés have plenty of zippy red-fruit character, but no tannin and, usually, a refreshing hit of palate-cleansing acidity, all of which makes them ideal for warm weather.

Is there anyone out there who doesn't like sparkling wine? Fizz can turn a picnic into an occasion, a pre-dinner drink into a celebration. It's as cheerful as a young puppy, and we love it for its optimism. The best (and most expensive) sparklers in the world come from Champagne–which isn't to say that every bottle bearing that famous name comes from this chilly region of northeastern France.

champagne and other sparkling wines

Plenty of countries outside Europe use the name as a catch-all term for anything with bubbles, and they're rarely as good as the genuine stuff, so be careful.

Champagne was invented over 300 years ago by a monk, Dom Pérignon, who lived in an abbey in the Marne Valley. It was so cold there in the fall and winter that wines often hadn't finished fermenting when they were bottled. When spring came, fermentation would start again, the wines filled with gas from the reaction, and bottles would explode. Dom Perignon didn't discover how to get fizz into the bottles (as is sometimes claimed), but he did find a way of controlling it and bottling the wines so that they stayed stoppered under pressure.

The monk of the Marne's other claim to fame is that he was the first person to realize that blending different grape varieties gives a more balanced wine than bottling them separately. Most champagnes are still made from a combination of the same three grapes: Chardonnay, Pinot Noir, and Pinot Meunier. (And yes, the last two are red—see page 120.)

Other places in the world make sparkling wine from the same grape varietals, but few of them have the same finesse as champagnes. That's because of the French region's chalky soil (which gives a distinctive minerally character, particularly to the Chardonnay) and its cool climate. Even in summer it's warm rather than hot there, which means the grapes ripen really slowly, giving maximum flavor while retaining plenty of acidity. This acidity makes the base wines almost undrinkable, but gives the finished fizz a freshness that keeps the drink light and lively in the mouth.

Really good champagne has a stream of super–fine bubbles. Not fat, lazy ones that expire halfway, but a vibrant line of them, rushing to the surface with energy.

Talking of fizz, take a look at it in your glass: really good champagne has a stream of super-fine bubbles. Not fat, lazy ones that expire halfway, but a vibrant line of them, rushing to the surface with energy.

The vast majority of champagne is "non-vintage," which means that it's a blend of lots of different wines from lots of different years, and is usually "brut" (dry), meaning it has next to no sugar in it. If you want something a bit sweeter, look for "sec," "demi-sec," or even "doux." There's no shame in it—plenty of people find brut champagne too dry for their taste.

Vintage champagne, produced only in the best years, is made from the grapes of just one year. The finest examples can age for decades, taking on an amazing complexity. Rosé champagnes are expensive, luxurious—and vary a lot in quality. The best are sensual and magnificent; the worst, a waste of money.

While nowhere else, strictly speaking, makes champagne, just about every country where wine grapes are grown makes sparkling wine of some description. Even France has good "non-champagne" options. Crémant wines from places like Limoux, the Loire, Alsace, and Burgundy are made using the same techniques as champagne, but from different grape varieties, and can offer excellent value for money, if not the cachet, of their world-famous neighbor.

Cavas from Spain tend to be approachable and good value rather than (with a few exceptions) actively good, though increasing numbers of New World producers are making great examples, often at bargain prices. The best are from New Zealand and Australia; there are also a few decent sparkling wines from South Africa, California, and even England.

If you go New World, pick with care. The cheapest fizzes are rarely worth bothering with, but if you move a few notches up the quality ladder, you will often get a wine that is the same quality as a non-vintage champagne for significantly less money.

grape varieties and wine styles

How is champagne made?

The classic *méthode champenoise* starts with a lowish-alcohol base wine, made the same way as an ordinary wine. The different varieties are blended, bottled, and a yeast and sugar mixture added. This starts a second fermentation, which does three things: it turns the newly added sugar into alcohol; it raises the alcohol to its final level; and it traps gas in the bottle, producing the fizz (and the pop of the cork).

After fermentation, the bottle has a small sediment of dead yeast cells in it (the lees). They don't look great, but it is the time that the bottle spends simply sitting there with this stuff inside it that gives champagne much of its characteristic toasty, brioche character. Before final bottling, this sediment is removed so only the flavor remains.

How does white wine come from red grapes?

Red wine's color comes from the time that the pressed wine spends in contact with its skins. If the red grapes are pressed gently and the juice removed from the skins immediately, the juice remains clear.

What is a Blanc de blancs?

A white champagne made only from white grapes, i.e. Chardonnay. A Blanc de noirs (rarer) is made only from Pinot Noir and Pinot Meunier.

Can you age champagne?

Vintage champagnes, definitely, provided the storage conditions are right (see page 226). Non-vintages are designed to be drunk within a few years of release.

First of all, rid yourself of the idea that sweet wine equals bad wine. It's true that some cheap-and-cheerful wine styles (German Liebfraumilch, white Zinfandel) are pretty sugary, and it's equally true that many people start to explore wine with examples like this and then move on to drier styles.

sweet wines

That doesn't mean that all sweet wines are made at an unambitious level, or that once you've discovered the joys of dry wines you shouldn't drink anything sweet again. Sauternes and Vouvray (France), Tokaji (Hungary), and the great dessert wines of Germany and Austria are some of the finest expressions in the world of wine, and to boycott them is to miss out.

First of all, how do you make a "sticky"? Do you take an ordinary wine and add sugar to it? No. The classic way is to pick a grape that's so super-ripe and chock-full of sugar that even when you've turned enough of that sugar into alcohol to make your wine, there's still loads left to give the wine sweetness.

And how does a grape get to this turbo-charged level of super-ripeness? The answer is time. Many sweet wines are labeled "late harvest" (*vendange tardive* in French), and hang on the vine for much longer than grapes used to make "ordinary" wine, accumulating sugar ripeness as they do so. There are good examples of these golden, honeyed wines from Alsace to the tip of Africa.

Once a grape has passed maturity, though, its looks fade faster than those of a Hollywood starlet

with a drug problem. You can forget images of plump, firm-skinned grapes dangling in the sun; grapes for sweet wines are as brown and wrinkled as a deflated leather football. They might make some of the most gorgeous wines on the planet, but all their beauty is on the inside.

In fact, some of the grapes for the most expensive sweet wines look positively toxic, covered as they are in a gray, downy mold. This is the rather unattractively named "noble rot" (or botrytis if you want to be technical), and while it looks grim it is the key to producing wines like Sauternes and Tokaji.

Brought on by warmth and humidity (great botrytized-wine-producing areas are all by rivers or lakes where there's fog in the morning during the fall), the furry coating splits the skins and makes the grapes shrivel. In fact, one of the reasons that Sémillon is the most-used grape in Sauternes is that it has a thin skin, which allows the mold easy access. The result: shriveled grapes, amazing intensity, and concentrated sugar flavors.

This, in fact, is why great sweet wines are not cheap. While for dry wine you might get a couple of bottles from one vine, for top sweeties the equation is reversed: you need the fruit of several vines just to make one bottle. Intensity is everything.

So OK, they're rich and concentrated, but does this make them sickly to drink? Interestingly, no. Good dessert wine, at least, should have plenty of acidity to go along with its sweetness, so that it stays fresh as well as flavorful in your mouth and leaves you wanting more—not reaching for a glass of water. It's

Good dessert wine stays fresh as well as flavorful in your mouth and leaves you wanting more.

one of the reasons that naturally high-acid varieties like Riesling (Germany/Alsace), Chenin Blanc (Vouvray), or Sauvignon Blanc (which is added to Sémillon in Sauternes) make better bets for stickies than grapes like Chardonnay. Even so, acidity or not, these wines are often so rich that you're not likely to want to drink more than half a glass or so—which is one of the reasons they're often sold in half-bottles. They might appear expensive, but with top-end sweet wines you really do get a lot of bang for your buck.

Lighter-flavored sweet wines like Moscato d'Asti (which is sparkling) or Muscat de Beaumes-de-Venise can be a good match with desserts, but your more expensive, super-rich sweeties really require something powerful but savory, such as foie gras, pâté, or a pungent blue cheese. Mind you, if you're feeling indulgent, you can always just chill it down and sip it on its own—maybe with the odd square of high-cocoa-content chocolate. But only if you've been really, really good…

There's only one thing that stops most people from trying fortified wines, and that's prejudice. Too strong, too sweet, no good with food—none of it's true. The fact that terms like port and sherry have often been used in the past to describe any cheapo fortified drink fit for little more than cooking hasn't helped. The real stuff, though, is classy, elegant, has tons of tradition, and can offer great value for money.

fortified wines

PORT

Proper port comes only from the baking terraced vineyards of the Douro Valley in northern Portugal. With the sun flashing down onto the sheer valley sides, and the river meandering lazily at the bottom, it's one of the most beautiful and atmospheric places in the wine world. While the grapes are grown up-valley in the high, parched lands near the Spanish border, the port industry's headquarters is the busy town of Oporto. This city, which gives port its name, is where the wines are aged and, eventually, released to the world.

Port is basically ordinary table wine that has had a little grape spirit added to it part-way through the fermentation process. It is

sweet, rich, heady stuff that comes in a variety of styles. Young ports, like ruby, are cheerful and inexpensive, good for sipping on their own. Reserve ports or, better still, late-bottled vintage (LBV) ports are not as expensive as you might think—an affordable way of getting something classy—while aged tawnies also deliver a lot of quality for money.

Vintage port is the ultimate port expression, sitting right at the top of the tree. Majestic wines to be savored, they are the perfect indulgent partner for blue cheese, with undeniable class. Bear in mind that you need to know how to serve it (see page 229 for how to decant it) and also that these are wines capable of seriously long aging. Twenty years is nothing for a vintage port, and

anything less than ten years is almost certainly too young and could well be "tight" and unexpressive. All ports work with cigars to a degree, though LBV and vintage are the best bets.

SHERRY

For starters, forget the idea that all sherry is sweet and strong. Most sherries are actually dry and barely above wine strength. Fino (the classic dry white style) and manzanilla are only about 15% alcohol—the same as the average bottle of Zinfandel.

Fino and manzanilla are great with seafood or as a pre-dinner drink, and like all sherries should be served chilled in a decent-sized glass. Fino sherry is nutty, tangy, and intense. Chilled right down, I have yet to find a better match with pre-dinner nibbles, and its lack of bubbles means you won't get bloated. Manzanilla is similar to fino but a bit lighter, with a faint whiff of sea air. It's peerless with shrimp. The good news about both these styles is that they're always absolutely bone-dry.

Darker sherries like amontillados or olorosos are a bit more complicated because they can be dry or sweet—so scan the label carefully. Both are great for drinking on their own, but dry versions are also excellent with cold meats, game, and soups. They're stronger than table wine (usually about 18% alcohol), but they deliver such intensity of flavor that you don't need to drink a lot. If you're serving fairly flavorsome pre-dinner snacks, a chilled dry amontillado sherry (absolutely gorgeous—rich, nutty, and tangy) is a classy option and won't spoil if you keep it for a few weeks after opening.

Super-sweet, tar-black Pedro Ximénez sherries are among the most intense, flavor-packed wines in existence and are magnificent with big, salty, blue cheeses like Roquefort or, if you want to match sweet with sweet, ice cream.

MADEIRA

From a tiny volcanic island in the Atlantic off the North African coast, Madeira's big advantage is its ability to stay the same for years after you've opened the bottle. Also, like port and sherry, it delivers a lot of flavor. Madeiras vary in style from dry to super-sweet. The driest style is Sercial, which is positively austere when young and needs a good few years to come round. Verdelho and Bual are sweeter, and Malmsey is the richest of the lot. With its exotic spicy banana flavors, Malmsey works brilliantly with cake.

choosing
WINE

Whatever the occasion, the right glass of wine really makes a difference to your enjoyment. Whether it's lunch with the in-laws or a lazy picnic with friends, you'll find suggestions here.

Wine isn't a **special-occasion** drink any more. It's a civilized accompaniment to more or less **any meal** you fancy, and the midweek glass is ever more popular.

For school nights, I suggest wine styles that go with several dishes. That way, if you only drink a couple of glasses one night, what's left will do for the next meal (use a vacuum set to keep it fresh for a couple of days).

Chardonnay, for instance, is a wonderfully versatile white. If it's not too heavily oaked, it'll go with fish, chicken, pork, and most pasta dishes. The same goes for other fleshy whites such as Pinot Blanc and Chenin Blanc. Sauvignon Blanc, on the other hand, might be a good match with fish, salad, and some oriental cuisines, but because it's lighter and more aromatic it can struggle with white meats—likewise Pinot Grigio.

For reds, mid-weight wines like Pinot Noir and Rioja can work with everything from pasta to meaty fish, pork chops, and even chili. The same goes for young, unambitious Bordeaux. But open a big Cabernet Sauvignon or Shiraz and, unless you drink it all in one sitting, it could hang around for a while. (I'm assuming here that you don't eat steak every night!)

Because midweek food rarely takes more than half an hour to prepare, adjust your wine budget accordingly. Really cheap stuff might actually detract from your meal, but there's no point spending more than you have to. Chile, Argentina, and Portugal are good sources of decent, value-for-money reds; lean towards Australia and South Africa for whites.

A good addition to the midweek kitchen is bag-in-box wine. A three-liter box is usually cheaper than four bottles, you can have as much or as little as you want at a time, and the wine will stay fresh for several weeks.

weeknight supper

For reds, mid-weight wines like Pinot Noir and Rioja can work with everything from pasta to meaty fish, pork chops, and even chili. The same goes for young Bordeaux.

Friday night is the start of the weekend. You want a wine that isn't going to look at you reproachfully if you slug it back without really concentrating.

friday-night TV wine

This means simple and pleasurable rather than complex. Big, cheerful flavors are in, elegance and restraint are out. Most such wines come from places with lots of sun: Australia, California, and Chile are great at making luscious, upfront wines, jammed with fruit, and they do it at good prices. Since it's to be drunk mostly on its own, we're looking for wines that don't have tons of "structure"—which means soft tannins for red wines and low acidity for whites.

So for whites I would rule out high-acid varieties such as Sauvignon Blanc or Riesling. Instead, look for an Aussie or California Chardonnay or a South African Chenin Blanc, all of which will be as comforting as your sofa's cushions. And take note of how much oak a white wine has. Big, creamy examples with lots of toasty, vanilla oak flavors may be initially exciting, but drinking more than one glass can be an effort.

For reds I'd steer clear of Cabernet Sauvignon, unless you have a special favorite. Its strong tannins aren't what you want when you're drinking a wine on its own. Go for softer varieties like Shiraz/Syrah or Merlot.

Australia, again, is great for the former, but California, South Africa, and Chile are all doing great Syrah, too. For juicy Merlot, California is your safest bet. If you want something a little bit different, Argentina does some great swigging Malbec. If you simply have to have a Cabernet, go for Chile, which makes the softest, most approachable examples in the world.

The **joy** of barbecues is their ad hoc nature–the **relaxed feel** of eating outside coupled with the chance to **pile your plate high** with a variety of foods. Both elements will affect the sort of wines you serve. Let's take the "outdoors" bit first. What you want to drink at lunchtime when it's **baking hot** is different from early evening when it's cooling off.

barbecue

Generally speaking, the hotter it is, the more attractive light, refreshing white wines are going to be. So if it's hot, look for bottles with plenty of fresh, spritzy acidity and not too much weight. Sauvignon Blanc is perfect, but so are Riesling, Muscadet, Soave, and unoaked Chardonnay. (Keep the bottles chilled.) These wines might not be a perfect match with the food, but they're perfect with the weather; if you're serving salads, fish, or even chicken, they'll be OK.

Rosé wines, chilled right down, are perfect for the barbecue. Served cool, they are as crisp and refreshing as whites, but take on more weight as they warm up. Make sure they're dry.

As it cools off, red wines become more appealing. Soft, luscious examples like Pinot Noir, Merlot, Chilean Carmenère, Rioja, Malbec, or Beaujolais are a good bet. Some reds work really well chilled, too. Beaujolais, Loire Cabernet Francs, and Pinot Noirs are the classics.

The eclectic nature of barbecue food makes an across-the-board match impossible. I wouldn't get too hung up about this; go for general rather than perfect matches. Mid-weight whites like Chenin Blanc, lightly oaked Chardonnay, Sémillon, Verdelho, or Viognier will work with everything but the red meats. Mid-weight reds like Merlot, Argentine Malbec, Barbera, Grenache, southern French reds like Fitou, and young Rioja will be fine with pork, lamb, and burgers. Zinfandel can be good, too, but it tends to be high in

alcohol, so be careful if it's really hot. Save the bigger, more "classic" reds for formal sit-down cookouts, but even here I wouldn't go for anything too heavy unless it's fairly cool (or you're eating indoors).

There's no need to spend big with barbecues. The food is fun rather than classy, so budget accordingly—maybe just above your Wednesday-night wine.

Finally, remember that alcohol and sun is a potent combination, so offer plenty of water.

Sunday lunch (or dinner) is something of an in-between occasion. It's several steps up from the rush of midweek dinners, yet not so involved as a gastronomic blowout; the sort of meal that you want to feel is special, but not one you want to spend all day preparing.

sunday lunch

So if you're going to buy one bottle of decent wine a week, make it for Sunday lunch. Fine wine shows particularly well when it's not fighting with dozens of huge flavors in the food. Since typical Sunday lunches are simple roasts, they are fabulous for showing off a better-than-average bottle of wine.

CHICKEN AND PORK
Both suit whites and light reds. For characterful whites, it's hard to beat Burgundy's Chardonnays; spend a bit extra, as budget versions are rarely worth the money. Australia and New Zealand both do flavorsome (and increasingly elegant) Chardonnays, while Aussie Semillon is a good mouth-filler. If you're having white meat with creamy sauce, a bottle of Riesling is a great and characterful match. Australia's are the best of the New World, but my preference would be a dry wine from Alsace if you can find it.

If you fancy a red with your white meat, Pinot Noirs like red Burgundy (same rules on price apply as for white Burgundies) are best. Otherwise, go for a light- to mid-weight Italian red like Valpolicella or Chianti.

LAMB
A juicy Spanish red from Rioja or Ribera is a classic match, but lamb also goes well with red Bordeaux and Chianti. Again, paying a bit extra makes a big difference to the quality, so if you go Spanish, look for *reserva* (or *crianza*) on the label.

BEEF
Here you need the heavyweights: big Cabernet Sauvignons, Merlots, or Syrah/Shirazes. A decent Bordeaux has the most class, but if you want plenty of sweet blackcurrant fruit, Cabs from Chile, Argentina, South Africa, Australia, New Zealand, and California are all worth a look. For Syrah/Shiraz, Australia and the Rhône are classic areas. The former tend to be richer and also work well with game.

STEWS AND CASSEROLES
Look for cheerfully chunky red wines from the Douro in Portugal or the Côtes du Rhône or Châteauneuf-du-Pape in France. Aussie Grenache, Spanish Garnacha, and Italian Primitivo are decent bets, too.

dinner party

There are different levels of dinner party–from the relatively **informal** "friends over" to the full-on **five-star bash** that takes days to prepare. The way you approach your wine depends on how special the occasion is.

Whatever the event, though, these are occasions when going the extra few yards, not just in the level of the wines you serve, but also in the variety of bottles on offer, makes a big difference.

First, the groundwork—getting the quantity right. Each bottle holds six glasses of wine. If there are four of you, assume that you'll need one bottle for the starter and two bottles for the main course. Next, are you having sparkling wine to start? (This really gives an evening a lift, and needn't be that expensive.) Dessert wine? Port? If so, the first two will need to be chilled, while the port and perhaps your red wine may need decanting (see page 229).

When it comes to the expense of the wines served, this too depends on the occasion. I wouldn't ever go below the Sunday-lunch level. And if it's a long-lost cousin visiting from Australia, you'll need to show it's a big deal with at least one really good bottle.

The good news (for your budget, at least) is that if you're serving two bottles of wine with the main course they don't both have to be superstars. In fact, having one great wine and one good one can make for an interesting exercise in "compare and contrast"!

For sheer class, it's hard to beat the great areas of Europe: Bordeaux, Burgundy, Chianti, Rioja, and Barolo (for reds) and Burgundy, Alsace, and the Loire (for whites). At the mid- to upper-price levels, the Rhône, south of France, Chile, South Africa, Australia, and California all offer good value for money.

Making a success of a big event like this means making sure of two things: one, that there's plenty of fizz; and two, that it's drinkable. This might sound blindingly obvious, but it's amazing how many occasions run out of reception sparkly after one glass or expect their guests to toast the happy couple with something resembling fizzy floor cleaner.

weddings

For the pre-dinner reception sparkler, you'll need something dry. If you go for champagne, look for brut (dry) or extra dry (just off-dry) on the label. For after-dinner toasts, find a sweeter version (demi-sec).

However, unless you have a huge budget, I'd skip champagne. Yes, at the top level it's gorgeous, but at the lower end it's rotten value for money. Instead, try a premium cava (a good one should still be less than half the price of champers), a fizz from the New World (New Zealand is a particularly good source), or a bubbly from France that's not from the hallowed Champagne region. Crémants from Burgundy, Alsace, and the Loire can be really good value for money. Research is essential before buying big volumes, so make sure you try all your prospective candidates.

When it comes to the meal wines, follow the rules for a weeknight supper and look for something soft and palate-friendly at a decent price. California, Chile, South Africa, south of France, southern Italy, and Argentina should all be on your radar. Incidentally, if you're buying half a dozen cases from one place, you should be able to negotiate a discount.

As for quantities, I'd allow half a bottle of sparkly per person and about the same of wine for the meal. Thus, for ninety guests, I'd buy four 12-bottle cases of sparkling wine, maybe three cases of red wine and two of white. No guest ever complained that there was too much wine, but they'll grumble if there's too little.

Most venues mark up wine by 200–300%. You could supply your own wine, especially if it has been given as a gift. Many venues charge a corkage fee of around $10–12 for every bottle of yours that they open, so if you buy wine at, say, $15–20 a bottle, that becomes $25–32 with corkage. Do your figures carefully to see if you'll end up with a decent wine at the same price or cheaper than the house wine.

thanksgiving

With its riot of flavors at the dinner table, Thanksgiving is a time of exuberant abandon for your palate–both a liberation and a curse when it comes to getting the right wines.

PRE-DINNER FIZZ

If you really want to start the day with a bang, champagne or Buck's Fizz is a decadent start. For Buck's Fizz (champagne and orange juice), I'd use any cheap sparkling wine. If you want your fizz neat, go for a non-vintage brut (dry) champagne or a New World sparkler.

THE DINNER

If you're looking for the perfect "silver bullet" match for turkey with cranberry sauce, stuffing, and sweet potatoes, forget it—there isn't one. The flavors (from sweet through savory) are just too diverse—and that's before you get into optional extras like ham and ribs.

Now, while that does mean that you can't plonk one bottle down on the table and expect it to do the whole meal, it also takes a lot of the pressure off the event. Since there's no such thing as an across-the-board match, you can serve your guests a number of different wines and let them decide which they like most. It gives you the chance to stir up a bit of debate when it comes to your selection. (Given the rustic nature of the food, you don't need to go crazy on the quality. Sunday-lunch level and slightly above is fine.)

Your best bets for Thanksgiving matches are at the light-to-medium end of the red spectrum and the rounded, flavorful end of the white. For classic red matches, we're looking at Pinot Noir/red Burgundy or a decent Beaujolais. If you try the latter (and it's a good match), try to get one of the crus from a village like Fleurie, Morgon, or Moulin-à-Vent. They'll have more concentration than just an ordinary Beaujolais.

You can also try lighter examples of Syrah/Shiraz. Probably not the powerful, inky versions from Australia, but more flowery, red-fruited examples from northern Rhône areas like Crozes-Hermitage, or countries like Chile or South Africa can work nicely.

If you want to be patriotic, then the uniquely American Zinfandel not only flies the stars and stripes, but also works pretty well with Thanksgiving fare. White Zinfandel is too sweet, but the red version will be fine. Just keep an eye on the alcohol levels. Since it frequently gets up around the 15% mark, don't expect sparkling post-dinner conversation if your guests have gone through a couple of bottles.

When it comes to whites, look for dry Riesling or Chardonnay. Fumé Blanc (an all-American version of Sauvignon Blanc) is a slightly lighter alternative.

If you want to keep it local, seek out the whites from Sonoma County or the Central Coast, which are more elegant than those from the Central Valley.

party

To an extent, the best advice I can give for party wine is, "Make sure there's plenty of it." But I'd like to qualify that statement by adding, "Do make sure that it's drinkable." If you stock up with the cheapest stuff you can find, your guests will avoid it and you'll have to drink it yourself over the next few months.

If in doubt, find the cheapest wine on offer, add 30% to the price, and don't buy anything below that. Before charging off to the supplier, it's worth asking yourself the following questions.

• Is it an occasion that requires celebratory fizz? Consider Spanish cava or something from the New World. Cheap champagne is rarely worth the money.

• Is it a hot-weather party or a cool-weather one? In hot weather people tend to drink more white wine.

• Will there be food or not—and what sort? A big tray of lasagne, for instance, needs red wine.

• How many people are coming and how much are they likely to drink? Allowing one bottle per person will be more than enough, particularly given that many might bring a bottle of their own.

With your answers, work out how much wine you want to buy and, roughly, the proportion of red and white you'll need. Buy by the case where you can

(there's often a discount), and shop around to find a deal on something party-friendly.

After that, it's on to styles. Essentially, for parties, you want wine that is similar to that for Friday nights (see pages 134–135): simple, undemanding, with a decent whack of fruit and not too high in either tannin or acidity; something that slips down easily.

For whites, New World Chardonnay is a good choice (even with a fair bit of oak), as are Riesling, Viognier, South African Chenin Blanc, California Fumé Blanc, and Aussie Semillon.

For reds, you want opulence without heavy tannin. Portuguese reds can be a good budget option, but Syrah/Shiraz, Malbec, and Chilean Carmenère are also safe bets. If you have to have Cabernet, stick with the New World. Incidentally, since parties get hot, it's worth filling the bathtub with ice and water and keeping all your wine there, not just the whites.

You can get wine of some description anywhere from swanky specialized vinothèques to glitzy bars to spit-and-sawdust pubs, but how do you avoid the garbage?

bars and pubs

Take your cue from your surroundings. If it looks like the sort of place that serves six bottles of wine a year, the stock isn't likely to be either fresh or well kept, so drink something else. If it's a really good wine bar, the staff may have worthwhile recommendations of their own, so ask them. Keep your eyes peeled for promotions that cut the price of an expensive wine to an affordable level (rather than those aimed at offloading cheap stock).

Generally you want soft, fruit-forward, easy-to-drink wines, rather than "classical" clarets and Chablis, which have more tannins (red) or acidity (white). I usually find white wines easier to drink in bars, provided they're not too warm. New World Chardonnay is a decent white choice, though some cheap examples can be a bit sickly. Sauvignon Blanc is a refreshing palate-sharpener on hot days, but is usually too acidic for more than one glass; be prepared to switch unless you want indigestion. White Bordeaux (a blend of Sauvignon Blanc and Sémillon) can be easier on the stomach.

Great by-the-glass whites for me are Riesling, Gewürztraminer, or Tokay Pinot Gris from Alsace, but they aren't always easy to find. Pinot Grigio is more common (and varies from sprightly to nasty, so pick with care).

If you go the red route, New World Cabernets, Merlots, and Shirazes are soft and juicy, but also get rather heavy for repeat drinking. Spanish reds (Tempranillo or Monastrell) or lighter Italians (Valpolicella and Barbera) are a good alternative, as is Beaujolais if it's a decent example.

This is arguably the hardest of all the categories to get right, since its success depends as much on your attitude as the actual wine you order. That's why it's really important to talk to your date about his or her preferences before you order. They may well not have strong opinions either way, but it really helps to know if, say, they don't like Chardonnay.

hot date

Once likes and dislikes have been safely worked out, it's on to deciding how much to spend. This, in a sense, is the tough bit. After all, we are all capable of ordering a less-than-brilliant wine from a wine list, but if we do it by choosing the cheapest on the menu, then we can fairly stand accused of being stingy.

As a general rule of thumb, take the price of the house wine, double it, and add a bit. At that level you should still be some way below the super-expensive wines (which could lay you open to charges of being flash), but safely into some pretty good stuff. (If you want to order Old World classics like Bordeaux and Burgundy, it helps if you know which vintages or producers to go for—you don't want to be lost in silent contemplation at the start of your date.)

At this price, the wine ought to speak for itself, but even if it's a bit disappointing, you can't be blamed. Having sought a consensus on what to choose at the start and then spent a decent amount on trying to achieve it, you have really done your best. And on a hot date you can't really ask for anything more.

DO

Start your date by ordering a couple of glasses of good champagne. It instantly gives the evening that special feel—and, because of its bubbles, fizz lowers inhibitions more quickly, helping conversation flow.

Consider more expensive wines from cheaper countries—they tend to be soft, rich, and flavorful. While not always a classic match, they are often extremely good value, and are very likeable.

DON'T

Buy the cheapest wines on offer, even if your date isn't a wine buff, or spend ages agonizing over the wine list (unless your date is a wine lover).

Gifting success depends not so much on spending a **fortune** as getting a wine that will **suit** the people you're buying it for.

wine gifts

For instance, while a wine buff isn't likely to be impressed with a cheap bottle of easy-drinking plonk, there's absolutely no point in buying *cru classé* Bordeaux for someone who only ever drinks wine in front of the TV. Likewise, if you're taking wine along to a barbecue, you need to decide whether the bottle is intended for consumption at the event or as a separate present to be drunk later by the hosts.

If you're buying wine as a present for people who drink wine regularly but aren't experts, the key is to find a wine style they like, then consider spending up to twice as much as they usually would, to get a wine that is guaranteed to deliver. You'll increase your chances of success if you avoid the supermarket in favor of somewhere with staff who can give you decent recommendations.

Having said all that, you can also go down the luxury-item route by buying less usual bottles like champagne, dessert wines, or fortifieds. These make great gifts, because people often like them, but tend not to buy them for themselves regularly. The inclusion of these luxury wines turns any meal into an occasion, and they'll probably think of you when they pop the cork.

The best value for money comes from non-vintage champagne from a good name, and late-bottled vintage port, which gives real after-dinner class without breaking the bank. Dessert wines are well priced, considering how much work goes into them.

BOTTLE-BUYING TIPS

Bottles of port and champagne often come in their own carton, which makes them both easier to wrap and better-looking than a bottle on its own. The same goes for spirits. Obviously it's not wine, but if you buy a bottle of spirits for someone make sure that they like the style you're buying.

Now, there are some occasions when only a chilled six-pack of beers will do, but equally there are times when wine is not just a good alternative, but is the best choice. If you're at an important game, a carefully selected bottle can make the day—whoever wins.

sports occasions and picnics

Tailgate parties are a part of American sporting life, and although baseball and beer seem to go together, wine is often the perferred drink at the stadium. Chilled in the cooler, it can be most welcome at a baseball game, whether it's to watch two of the major-league teams or enjoy a lazy Saturday afternoon at the local diamond. And it can be wonderfully warming before, during, or after a football game on a cold winter's afternoon. In any case, though, make sure you don't drink and drive home after the game.

Fizz is always a great start for a summer picnic and can really make it an occasion to remember. If you don't want to indulge with champagne, New Zealand makes great sparkling wine or, at the lower end, cava from Spain is a fair alternative. English sparkling, too, can be excellent.

For picnic whites, keep it light and zippy— Sauvignon Blanc, Riesling, and Soave are refreshing when drunk outside in the sun. For reds, avoid the heavy stuff. Beaujolais is good chilled and juicily appealing, but young Rioja and Pinot Noir work fine, too. Finally, as with barbecue wines, rosé is a great (and underrated) alternative.

PICNIC EXTRAS

A few accessories can make all the difference. For instance, you absolutely have to have a coolbox if you're taking wine on a picnic. There's nothing worse than lukewarm champers or white wine. A chiller sleeve to put around opened bottles isn't a bad idea, either—even for reds, if it's really hot.

As for glasses, if you don't have a five-star hamper that will allow you to transport real glasses safely, see if you can get some non-glass wine glasses. There's something incredibly depressing about drinking wine out of plastic stacker-cups, and even plastic wine glasses are a big improvement.

food and
WINE

Get the right bottle together with the right food, and it will
shine. This chapter should point you in the direction of a
good wine–food match, whatever your favorite cuisine.

Many people find ordering wine in a restaurant a somewhat intimidating experience. Fortunately, the scenario of giant, incomprehensible wine list and snooty waiter happens less and less, and if you follow the suggestions below you should do well.

navigating the wine list

Ask the waiter

Good wine waiters are usually pleased to offer suggestions. Tell them what you're all eating, what you generally like, give them a price, and see what they come up with. Remember, this is their job! Don't be talked into spending more than you want to.

Look for familiar faces

If the restaurant doesn't have a wine specialist and your waiter looks clueless, look for brand names, grape varieties, or even countries that you like to drink.

Try before you buy

A lot more restaurants are offering a decent selection of wines by the glass. If you try a selection with your appetizers (or before sitting down to eat), you'll be able to order bottles of your favorites with confidence. Single glasses can also be a fantastic way of keeping everyone happy if, for instance, your table of four orders red meat, white meat, vegetarian, and fish.

Look for clues on the wine list

Nowadays more and more wine lists include helpful descriptions of the flavors of the wines and even, in some cases, food-matching suggestions.

Avoid house wines

The fact that house wines are the cheapest wines on the list doesn't, by any stretch, make them the best value. Typically, they're very, very cheap wines that have been hugely marked up, and I've rarely had even a halfway decent one. A good benchmark is to find the price of the house wine, add 50%, and start looking around that level.

Consider safety first

If you are struggling, certain wines are always solid and reliable (although not necessarily the best on the list). You won't go far wrong with Chilean Cabernet Sauvignon, California Merlot, Australian Chardonnay and Shiraz, and New Zealand Sauvignon Blanc.

Classic French food is usually a fairly simple mix of ingredients, so it is easy for it to work in harmony with the wine, allowing both to shine at once.

french

So if you're ever going to splash out and spend big in a restaurant, this is the type of food with which to do it. Obviously, in the suggestions below you could substitute, say, a California Cabernet for a Bordeaux. But I've stuck with French recommendations for two good reasons: French wines are generally very food-friendly; and your average French restaurant doesn't sell many wines from anywhere else!

SEAFOOD AND FISH

Oysters, shrimp, and *moules marinières* are at their best with zingy northern French whites like Chablis, Muscadet, and Sauvignon Blancs from the Loire. For light, white fish, simply grilled, go with the flinty Sauvignon Blancs of Sancerre. Creamy sauces need something more substantial, like a white Burgundy or an Alsace Riesling. Meaty fish like monkfish can work with lighter reds such as Pinot Noir, decent Beaujolais, or Loire Cabernet Franc, as well as bigger Burgundies.

CASSEROLES

If there's wine in the sauce, then it's usually a good bet to use the same wine to accompany the casserole. Thus *coq au vin* and *boeuf bourguignon* both work with

simple Burgundy, though the beef can also stand up to more substantial "comfort" wines, such as reds from the Rhône or the south of France. There's no need to spend a lot on wine for these hearty dishes.

BEEF

Depends a bit on how it's cooked and how good the cut is. Simple *steak frites* or more rustic joints are good either with cheap Bordeaux, Côtes du Rhône, or southern French reds. For top-quality filet, you want as good a wine as you can afford from Bordeaux, Burgundy, or classic Rhône areas like Côte Rôtie.

CHICKEN

In a salad, go with medium-bodied whites like Chablis or simple Burgundy. If it's roasted, find a good wine to show the chicken off, like a decent white Burgundy. If you're eating really good meat (say, *poulet de Bresse*), red Burgundies work, too.

CHEESE AND PÂTÉ

Sweet Sauternes is a nailed-down classic match with both foie gras and Roquefort. For big, pungent (or smoky) cheeses, try Gewürztraminer from Alsace; for Brie, Camembert, et al, white Burgundy is your man!

italian

Italian food is justifiably among the most popular in the world. Its riot of colors and flavors, while retaining a suitably homey feel, makes it comfort food par excellence. It is also exceptionally wine-friendly, and most dishes work pretty well even if the wine match isn't perfect.

PASTA

It's all about the sauce. For seafood-based pasta, you can try just about any white that doesn't have lots of oak in it. Pinot Grigio, Sauvignon Blanc, Chablis, or a lightish unoaked Chardonnay will all be fine.

For aromatic, fragrant pasta sauces like pesto, you need a wine that won't override the flavors. So gently flavored Italian whites like Gavi or Soave can work, as can a Catarrato from Sicily. Outside Italy, Albariño, New World Riesling, a California Fumé Blanc, or mid-weight Chardonnay are fine.

For carbonara-type creamy sauces, you need a bit of structure to cut through the cream, but not too much fruit flavor, which may clash. I'd recommend either the same sort of whites that match the pesto, or lighter reds such as a Montepulciano, a cheap Bordeaux, or a Cabernet Franc from the Loire.

For meatier sauces like bolognese, try the more heavyweight Italian reds. Chianti is a good match, but avoid the cheapest. Primitivo is a good (and cheaper)

alternative. Otherwise, try any gutsy wine: Cabernet Sauvignon, Syrah/Grenache blends (say, from the southern Rhône Valley), Zinfandel, or Chilean Malbec.

PIZZA

With its mix of flavors, pizza is not an easy dish with which to match wine. Go for wines with gentle rather than overt flavors and of no more than medium weight. Even pizzas with lots of toppings tend not to be heavy, and a big red wine will stamp all over them. For whites, a fresh Italian like Soave or an unoaked Chardonnay work with most; for reds, Barbera and Montepulciano (from Italy), a southern French Roussillon, or Fitou, or young Rioja, are safe bets.

OTHER CLASSICS

Meaty lasagne and ravioli follow the same rules as bolognese. For vegetarian versions, take the carbonara route. For veal, Soave is the lighter match. If it's served with a heavier sauce, try a Pinot Noir.

As with all types of food, but especially Asian cuisines, there is no "one bottle suits all" match for Chinese food. If you're in a group, pick a selection of bottles and try small amounts of different wines with each dish.

chinese

The good news is that Chinese food does offer some genuinely good matches. Sauvignon Blanc (or champagne) works with egg rolls and most seafood dishes, while lusher whites such as Chardonnay or Sémillon go with bigger-flavored chicken or pork dishes. Avoid anything very dry, like Sancerre or Chablis—the sweetness of many Chinese dishes means the wine needs a little lushness to it.

Chinese food is rarely hot, which means red wines can play a part. As with the whites, New World wines usually make a good match. Duck dishes are a classy partner with New Zealand Pinot Noir, while staples like beef and black bean sauce work with bigger, sweeter New World wines such as Chilean Carmenère, California Merlot, and Aussie Shiraz.

Gewürztraminer is often suggested for Chinese food, but its key flavor, litchis, may clash horribly. Will your dish work with a side dish of litchis? If not, stick with a more neutral Pinot Blanc or Chardonnay.

With its purity of flavor, Japanese food can offer good wine matches, particularly if you're having sushi. The Japanese often drink sake with it, and for me the best match is the wine that is closest to sake stylistically: bone-dry, savory fino or manzanilla sherry.

japanese

If you prefer non-fortified wine, the key is to go dry. New World whites tend to have too much sweetness of fruit for sushi, so stick to Europe and "classic" regions like Sancerre, Chablis, or Burgundy, where the flavors tend to be flinty and chalky. Dry (brut) champagne can be an inspired match with sushi, particularly if it's a good, chalky Blanc de blancs. For teppanyaki, amontillado sherry can do the trick.

Meatier Japanese dishes obviously require red wine, but nothing too enormous that might destroy the flavors. So, provided what you've ordered isn't too spicy, medium-bodied European reds are likely to be best. Young Bordeaux or Burgundies work well, and so can Chianti, Rioja, and Loire Cabernet Francs. If you want to go New World, a Kiwi or Aussie Pinot Noir (from Tasmania if possible) is probably your best bet.

For anything with lots of dominant strong flavors that are "difficult" for wine (for example, Japanese pickles, wasabi, and sesame oil), you might want to go native and try that sake!

The biggest problem with matching wine
to Indian food comes down to one thing:
heat. If you are addicted to searing dishes
like vindaloo, you'll just have to accept that
your choice is, to put it mildly, limited.

indian

If you prefer creamier or medium-spiced dishes, then
things get easier. If in doubt, the safest bet for Indian
food is white wine. Since the dominant flavor in
Indian cooking tends to be the sauce rather than the
meat, it's perfectly possible to have red meat and
white wine. There are two routes to go down: either
find a big, pungent white that will wrestle with the
food head-on (like an Alsace Gewürztraminer), or go
for something neutral that acts as a "straight man" to
the food and soothes the spiciness.

Lush Tokay Pinot Gris or Pinot Blancs (from Alsace)
are good bets here. For creamier dishes like korma or
passander, Rieslings are a decent match; for fish
curries, try New Zealand or South African Sauvignon
Blanc. White Rhône also works with many dishes.

If you fancy something unusual, big dessert wines
like Tokaji work surprisingly well. They have the
lushness to stand up to pretty hot dishes and plenty
of cleansing acidity to keep the mouth fresh.

With its myriad spices and penchant for chilies, it's difficult to get a perfect wine match with Thai food. The most important thing is to gauge the heat of the dish. If you crunch down on a green chili, don't expect a glass of dry red wine to bring you much relief.

thai

Few Thai dishes suit red wine, so head straight for the white section of the wine list, whatever you're eating. Why? The aromatic nature of the dishes is better suited to the flavor profiles of white grapes. Red wines either override the spices completely or clash with them. Second, white wines have no tannin, which dries your mouth and exaggerates any heat in food. Not only that, but they do have higher acidity, which can help to freshen your palate and counteract any heat in the dish just as well as beer can.

A little sweetness isn't by any means a bad thing, either, so my top recommendations for Thai food would be German Riesling (Spätlese or Kabinett, if they've got it), juicy, aromatic Sauvignon Blancs from New Zealand, and apricot-scented Viogniers. For hot, but light dishes (say pork, chilies, and basil), try a fresh, neutral Soave or Pinot Blanc. For meatier dishes, go with an Alsace Tokay Pinot Gris.

greek and lebanese

The classic cuisine of Greece and Lebanon features a mixed selection of starters (meze), followed by meat or fish. With its emphasis on natural ingredients and simple, fresh flavors, wine matching here is a dream.

Why? There aren't too many conflicting tastes to get in the way, and the dominant flavors, garlic and herbs, are far easier to match with wine than, say, chilies and lemon grass.

For meze, a good, crisp white wine is the best starter. A modern white Rioja or Albariño from Galicia in Spain; a Loire Sauvignon Blanc; a herby Catarrato from Sicily; a cool Soave; even a crisp Portuguese white—all will work with the majority of Greek and Lebanese starters. You can even try an unoaked Chardonnay with lamb meze if they've been drizzled with lemon juice, and the wine could then continue with the main course if you've ordered grilled fish.

For meats, again, the simplicity of flavors makes matching reds comparatively simple. Sweetly fruited wines aren't likely to be a great match with savory, herby flavors, so look in Europe or cooler areas of the New World. Bordeaux, Rioja, and Ribera del Duero are good, as are Chianti and Fitou. If you want an Aussie Cabernet, try Western Australia.

mexican

With its robust flavors and cheerful spices, there's absolutely no point in getting too fancy when it comes to matching wines with most Mexican food. The key here is to keep it simple.

With chunky food like chicken burritos, you're looking at the soft, round, and full-flavored end of the spectrum rather than delicate and aromatic, which leads us once again to Chenin Blanc, Chardonnay, and/or Sémillon country. A bit of oak is fine, but remember that anything heavily wooded will increase any heat in the dish.

For seafood fare featuring, say, shrimp, limes, and chili, Rieslings can be an inspired match, and the acidity will freshen your palate as effectively as beer.

For chunky red meat dishes, you need a wine that is not too tannic, so won't exaggerate heat in the food. This rules out many Cabernet Sauvignons, but there are still plenty of wines out there with attitude that work well. Southern French reds (Rhône Villages, Languedoc) have a bit of grunt, as does Syrah/Shiraz.

For me, the best match with tortillas, tacos, et al, is California's own Zinfandel. Big and lush, it manages to be spicy without being aggressive, and soft without being flabby. Well worth a look—just don't confuse it with sweet, white Zinfandel.

food and wine

While with seafood it's broadly true that if you order anything **chilled** and **white**, you won't be too far off the mark, some matches are indisputably better than others; there's a **world** of difference between a delicate lemon sole and a meaty tuna steak.

seafood

Lobster and shrimp work really well with fresh, delicate whites like Muscadet. For simple fish dishes (without strong sauces), you can't go wrong with a Sauvignon Blanc, particularly from Sancerre. Fresh and steely, it's a classic match with the likes of sole.

For meatier fish like halibut and sea bass, you need a bigger wine, and while you can get away with a good Sauvignon Blanc, a lightly oaked (or unoaked) Chardonnay, like a Chablis, will nearly always carry the day. For seriously meaty fish like tuna and shark, you want biggish (lightly or unoaked) Chardonnays from countries like Australia or South Africa, or even light reds like Pinot Noir, Beaujolais, or Cabernet Franc.

If you have to pick one wine to go with a variety of different seafood dishes, Chablis is probably your best bet. It's fresh, but with reasonable body.

This is some of the **toughest** food to get a good wine match with. For starters, it's non-traditional, so there are no **classic** matches; and its tendency to throw unusual tastes together can make it hard to predict **flavors** just by looking at the menu.

fusion food

However, since most fusion restaurants tend to be fairly serious establishments, they usually have a wine waiter—so don't be shy about asking for advice.

Although you can usually come up with something reasonable by a process of elimination (if a dish is Thai-influenced, you can follow the rules on page 167, for example), for me the key is not to get too hung up on the search for perfection. Fusion food is fun, and you need to grab that spirit of adventure. Be like the chef: experiment, and enjoy yourself.

A fair few fusion dishes mix big flavors to make an even bigger combination. This can be too much for most wine styles, but sherry (yes, sherry) can work really well for these power-plates if you get the right style. Try manzanilla or fino with fish, amontillado with game, and oloroso with red meat.

cooking with WINE

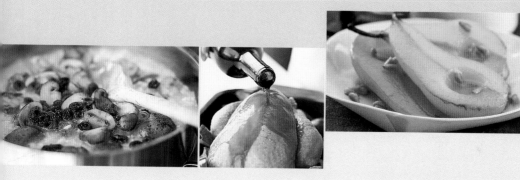

Don't restrict wine to your glass—it's an essential ingredient in many classic recipes. Here, you'll find old favorites as well as new creations, all bringing the taste of wine to your plate.

Cut the meat into very large chunks–long, slow cooking tenderizes it perfectly. Served with boiled potatoes and green vegetables, it's a good dish for a crowd.

beef braised in red wine

Pour the wine into a large saucepan and bring to a boil. Boil hard until reduced by half (leaving 3 cups). Let cool completely.

Cut the meat into 2-inch pieces. Put in a large plastic bag with the onions, carrots, celery, bay leaves, thyme, peppercorns, and allspice. Pour in the cooled wine. Shake the bag to mix, then seal the bag and put it in a large bowl to marinate in the refrigerator overnight.

Open the bag and pour the contents into a colander set over a bowl. Separate the meat from the vegetable mixture and pat the pieces dry with paper towels. Reserve the wine.

Heat the olive oil in the casserole dish on top of the stove and brown the meat well in batches. Return the meat to the dish, then stir in the vegetable mixture, the cooled wine, and the tomato paste. Add enough stock to cover the meat and vegetables. Bring to a boil, reduce the heat, then cover and cook in a preheated oven at 325°F for 2–3 hours until very tender, adding extra stock if it evaporates too quickly. Alternatively, simmer gently on top of the stove for 2–3 hours.

Using a slotted spoon, transfer the meat to a bowl. Discard the bay leaves. Pour the sauce into a food processor and blend until smooth (the sauce will look pale, but will darken when reheated). Add salt and pepper to taste. The sauce should be quite thick—if not, boil to reduce it. Stir the meat back into the sauce, reheat, sprinkle with parsley, and serve with boiled potatoes and steamed cabbage.

Recommended wine match A gutsy red: Aussie Barossa Shiraz, Italian Barolo or Brunello, Californian Cabernet Sauvignon, northern Rhône.

2 bottles Barolo or other good-quality red wine, 750 ml each

3 lb. stewing beef such as chuck or bottom round, well trimmed

2 onions, coarsely chopped

2 carrots, chopped

1 celery stalk, chopped

2 bay leaves

2 large sprigs of thyme

6 peppercorns

2 allspice berries, crushed

3 tablespoons olive oil

2 tablespoons tomato paste

about 1½ quarts beef stock

sea salt and freshly ground black pepper

To serve

chopped fresh flat-leaf parsley

boiled potatoes

steamed cabbage

a large flameproof casserole dish

SERVES 6–8

This dish must be made in advance in order for the flavors to develop and the sauce to taste rich and delicious. If you are reheating it from cold, put into a preheated oven at 350°F for 35 minutes.

wine–marinated daube of beef

Put the beef, wine, bay leaves, salt, and pepper into a large bowl, cover, and chill for 24 hours, turning the beef in its marinade from time to time.

Drain the beef, reserving the marinade, and pat dry with paper towels. Heat 2 tablespoons of the olive oil in the casserole dish, add the onions and garlic, and cook gently for 8 minutes. Sprinkle with the flour and stir. Add the marinade liquid a little at a time, stirring constantly. Add the capers, olives, tomatoes, and orange zest and simmer while you prepare the beef.

Put the remaining olive oil into a skillet and heat until hot. Dust the beef with flour and add to the skillet. Fry until brown on all sides, then transfer to the casserole. Put a few tablespoons of juice from the casserole back into the skillet and stir to scrape up any meaty bits. Add the juice and bits back to the casserole.

Cover with a lid and cook in a preheated low oven at 275°F for 2 hours. Remove from the oven and add the carrots and mushrooms. Return the casserole to the oven and cook for another hour.

Remove the beef to a board, slice thickly, and serve on heated dinner plates. Stir the parsley into the sauce and spoon the sauce and vegetables over the beef. Serve with egg noodle pasta, tossed in parsley and butter, or with boiled potatoes.

Recommended wine match Big smooth reds: Ribera del Duero with some bottle age, Australian McLaren Vale Shiraz, Bordeaux, Chianti, Duoro (Portugal).

4 lb. boneless rump roast

1 bottle white wine, 750 ml

2 bay leaves

¼ cup olive oil

2 onions, sliced

2 garlic cloves, chopped

3 tablespoons all-purpose flour, plus extra for dusting

1 tablespoon drained capers

4 oz. black olives, such as Niçoise or kalamata, pitted, about 1 cup

1 can chopped tomatoes, 14 oz.

grated zest of ½ unwaxed orange

8oz. baby carrots

4 oz. button mushrooms

a large bunch of flat-leaf parsley, chopped

sea salt and freshly ground black pepper

egg noodle pasta or boiled potatoes, to serve

a large flameproof casserole dish

SERVES 6

This recipe is a simpler version of the traditional Tuscan *porchetta* (whole pigs stuffed and roasted in wood ovens) often sold sliced and crammed into buns in food markets. Use as much rosemary as you can so the sweet pork flesh will be suffused with its pungent aroma.

pork loin roasted with rosemary and garlic

Ask the butcher to bone the loin, but to give you the bones. Also ask him to remove the skin and score it to make the crackling. Turn the loin fat side down. Make deep slits all over the meat, especially in the thick part.

Put the garlic and chopped rosemary in a food processor with at least 1 teaspoon each of salt and pepper, and blend to a paste. Push the paste into the slits in the meat and spread the remainder over the surface of the meat. Roll up and tie with kitchen twine, placing some long sprigs of rosemary along its length. Weigh the meat and calculate the cooking time, allowing 25 minutes per pound. If desired, wrap in plastic wrap and leave in the refrigerator for several hours to deepen the flavor.

When ready to cook, heat the olive oil in a skillet, unwrap the pork, if necessary, and brown all over. Set in a roasting pan and pour the wine over the pork. Tuck in the remaining rosemary sprigs. Place the bones in another roasting pan convex side up. Rub the pork skin with a little olive oil and salt. Drape the skin over the pork bones. Place the pan of crackling on the top shelf of a preheated oven, and the pork on the bottom or middle shelf. Roast at 450°F for 20 minutes, then reduce the heat to 400°F, and roast for the remaining calculated time, basting the pork loin every 20 minutes.

Rest the pork in a warm place for 15 minutes before carving into thick slices. Serve with shards of crunchy crackling and the pan juices.

Recommended wine match The fragrant herbs mean a white; an Italian like Gavi di Gavi or a good Soave. Go upmarket with an older (dry) Riesling.

4 lb. bone-in pork loin roast

4 large garlic cloves

¼ cup chopped fresh rosemary

a bunch of rosemary sprigs

2 tablespoons extra virgin olive oil, plus extra for rubbing

⅓ cup dry white wine

sea salt and freshly ground black pepper

kitchen twine

SERVES 6

cooking with wine

This rustic Italian recipe is a simple way to give ordinary chicken a taste of the wild hills of Tuscany. The secret is in the reduction of the wine and the long, slow cooking. The sauce is very dark and rich, so serve with plain fare such as polenta or a salad to follow.

etruscan hunter's chicken

Wash and dry the chicken joints. Mix the garlic, chopped rosemary, 1 teaspoon salt, and 1 teaspoon pepper in a small bowl. Rub well into the flesh, especially the cut sides. Cover and let marinate for at least 2 hours.

Meanwhile pour the wine into a nonreactive pan, add the rosemary sprigs, and boil hard until reduced by half, then set aside and let cool.

Heat the olive oil in the casserole dish and add the pancetta, onion, carrot, and celery and fry until just beginning to color. Add the chicken pieces and turn in the vegetables, cooking until just colored.

Add the sage leaves, then strain the infused white wine through a strainer into the casserole dish, scraping up any sticky brown sediment from the bottom of the dish. Add a little stock to bring the liquid up to just cover the joints. Bring to a boil, then half-cover and simmer very gently for about 45 minutes, turning the chicken in the liquid every now and then—the sauce will gradually reduce. Lift the chicken onto a plate.

Add the livers to the sauce, then purée with a hand-held blender or in a food processor, or pass through a mouli (vegetable mill). Return the pieces of chicken (and the sauce, if necessary) to the casserole dish. Add the olives and continue cooking for 10 minutes until heated through. If the sauce is a little thick, add a little more stock. Serve with polenta or a salad to follow.

Recommended wine match White meat, but a dark sauce, so mid-weight red is best. A slightly older Burgundy would be perfect.

1 medium chicken, about 3½ lb., and 2 chicken livers

4 large garlic cloves, finely chopped

1 tablespoon finely chopped rosemary

1 bottle medium dry white wine, 750 ml

2 sprigs rosemary

6–8 tablespoons olive oil

3 oz. pancetta, finely diced

1 onion, finely chopped

1 carrot, finely chopped

1 stalk of celery, finely chopped

6 fresh sage leaves

about 1¼ cups vegetable stock

2¼ cups juicy black olives, pitted

sea salt and freshly ground black pepper

polenta or salad, to serve

a large flameproof casserole dish

SERVES 4–6

This classic French dish is ideal for a dinner party as it tastes even better the day after it's made, which means you can make it in advance. The French would always use a local wine.

coq au vin

Put 2 tablespoons of the flour in a shallow dish and season with salt and pepper. Dip the chicken breasts in the flour to coat. Heat 2 tablespoons of the olive oil in a large lidded skillet or deep casserole and fry the chicken breasts for 2–3 minutes on each side until lightly browned.

Remove the chicken from the pan, discard the oil, and wipe the pan with paper towels. Return to the heat and add the remaining oil. Add the bacon and the shallots and fry until lightly browned. Stir in the garlic, then return the chicken to the pan. Put the brandy in a small saucepan and heat it until almost boiling. Set it alight with a long kitchen match and carefully pour it over the chicken. Let the flames die down, then add the thyme and bay leaf and enough wine to just cover the chicken. Bring back to simmering point, then reduce the heat, half-cover the pan, and simmer very gently for 45 minutes. (If making this dish ahead of time, take the pan off the heat after 30 minutes, let it cool, then refrigerate overnight.) Add the mushrooms and cook for another 10–15 minutes.

Remove the chicken and keep warm. Using a slotted spoon, remove the shallots, bacon, and mushrooms. Increase the heat and simmer to reduce by half. If the sauce needs thickening, mash the butter and remaining flour until smooth, then add gradually, beating well after each addition.

Return the shallots, bacon, and mushrooms to the pan. Add salt and pepper, to taste. Cut each chicken breast into 4 slices and arrange on warmed serving plates. Spoon the sauce over the chicken and sprinkle with parsley. Serve with creamy mashed potato or tagliatelle.

3 tablespoons all-purpose flour

6 large skinless, boneless chicken breasts

3 tablespoons olive oil

4 oz. chopped bacon or pancetta

10 oz. shallots, chopped into even-size pieces

2 garlic cloves, thinly sliced

¼ cup brandy

3 sprigs of fresh thyme

1 bay leaf

1 bottle dry fruity red wine, such as Côtes du Rhône-Villages, Gigondas, or a fruity young Syrah, 750 ml

8 oz. small button mushrooms

1 tablespoon butter, softened (optional)

¼ cup chopped fresh flat-leaf parsley

sea salt and freshly ground black pepper

creamy mashed potato or tagliatelle, to serve

SERVES 6

Recommended wine match Red Burgundy or Côte du Rhône.

This is one of the easiest supper dishes imaginable. It takes less time to cook than a supermarket ready meal and it is much more delicious. You can use any dry white wine to make it, but Viognier—an exotic, slightly scented grape variety that thrives in southern France and, nowadays, in California—has a lovely rich quality. Unoaked or lightly oaked Chardonnay will also work well.

sautéed chicken with white wine, pea, and tarragon sauce

Heat the olive oil in a large skillet, then add the pancetta. Fry for a couple of minutes until the fat starts to run. Add the chicken slices and fry, stirring occasionally, until lightly golden, for 4–5 minutes.

Add the onion to the pan and fry for 1–2 minutes. Add the wine and peas and cook until the wine has reduced by about two-thirds. Reduce the heat and stir in the tarragon, sour cream, and black pepper to taste. Heat gently until almost bubbling.

Remove the pan from the heat. Transfer the sautéed chicken to 2 warm plates, spoon over the sauce, and serve immediately with steamed asparagus tips.

Recommended wine match A good fruity Chardonnay with a little oak on it from California or Australia.

1 tablespoon olive oil

3½ oz. pancetta or bacon, chopped

2 skinless, boneless chicken breasts, cut into thin slices

1 small onion, very finely chopped

⅔ cup full-bodied dry white wine, such as Viognier

1 cup fresh or frozen peas

2 tablespoons finely chopped fresh tarragon leaves

about 4 generous tablespoons sour cream or crème fraîche

freshly ground black pepper

steamed asparagus tips, to serve

SERVES 2

Sea bass has the perfect texture for this delicious dish, which is perfect for a summer lunch under a vine-laden awning. Serve with lots of bread and use virgin olive oil, rather than extra virgin, as the latter is too powerful for the mildly acidic flavors of this dish.

sea bass in vinaigrette with capers and parsley

Working in 2 batches, put 1 cup of the wine and 1 cup cold water in a shallow pan such as a nonstick skillet. Add half the strips of lemon and orange zest, 1 of the shallots, half the parsley stalks, and salt. Add half the sea bass fillets and slowly bring to a gentle simmer, about 5 minutes. As soon as the liquid starts to bubble, take the pan off the heat and leave for 2 minutes. Transfer the fillets to a serving dish and keep them warm, while you repeat with the second batch, using 1 cup wine, 1 cup cold water, the remaining strips of zest, 1 shallot, the remaining parsley, and some salt.

Meanwhile, soak the remaining shallots in the vinegar for about 3 minutes. Drain off the vinegar into a bowl and use to make the dressing. Reserve the soaked shallots.

Add the sugar, salt, and pepper to the vinegar and beat in the olive oil, a little at a time. Mix in the shallots, capers, and parsley and pour over the fish fillets while they are still hot. Let cool and eat after 1–2 hours.

Recommended wine match With that sauce you need a neutral white wine from Spain or Italy—Rioja or Soave. Albariño might be an interesting match, too.

2 cups dry white wine

zest from 1 unwaxed lemon, peeled off in wide strips

zest from 1 unwaxed orange, peeled off in wide strips

3–4 large shallots or red onions, thinly sliced

a handful of parsley stalks

2 lb. sea bass fillets
(4–8, depending on size)

2 tablespoons white wine vinegar

½ teaspoon sugar

⅓ cup virgin olive oil

3 tablespoons capers, drained and rinsed

3 tablespoons fresh flat-leaf parsley leaves

coarse sea salt and freshly ground black pepper

SERVES 4

Monkfish makes an excellent alternative to a meaty roast, especially when it is served with a robust red wine gravy. It also makes an impressive entrée for a dinner party.

roast monkfish with pancetta, rosemary, and red wine gravy

Put the chopped rosemary in a bowl. Add 1 crushed garlic clove, the softened butter, salt, and pepper and beat well with a wooden spoon.

Lay out the monkfish fillets in pairs with the thin end of 1 fillet next to the thick end of the other. Spread the rosemary butter on one side of each fillet, then press each pair together and wrap them in the pancetta. Put 1 tablespoon of the olive oil in a shallow cast-iron pan or flameproof dish, then add the monkfish. Put the remaining garlic, the rosemary, and shallots around the monkfish, then drizzle over the remaining oil. Roast in a preheated oven at 400°F for 25 minutes, turning the shallots and garlic halfway through, until the pancetta is nicely browned.

Carefully remove the monkfish from the pan, lightly cover with foil, and set aside. Leaving the shallots and garlic in the pan, pour off all but 1 tablespoon of the oil and butter, then heat the pan over medium heat for 2 minutes, stirring. Pour in the wine and let it bubble until reduced by half. Add the stock, and continue to let it bubble until the gravy is reduced by half again. Strain the gravy through a fine-meshed strainer and return to the pan, with any juices that have accumulated under the fish. Reheat gently, then beat in the chilled butter. Adjust the seasoning, if necessary.

Cut the monkfish into thick slices, then divide among 4 or 6 plates. Serve with the gravy, sautéed potatoes, and mixed salad greens.

Recommended wine match A Pinot Noir, Merlot, or a Sangiovese-based Italian red like Chianti would go well with this dish.

1 tablespoon rosemary, very finely chopped

7 garlic cloves

4 tablespoons butter at room temperature, plus an extra 2 tablespoons, chilled and cubed

2 small monkfish tails, about 1 lb. each, skinned, boned, and each divided into 2 fillets

4 oz. very thinly sliced pancetta or bacon, rind removed

2 tablespoons olive oil

4 sprigs of rosemary

8 shallots, quartered

¾ cup full-bodied fruity red wine, such as Merlot or Argentinian Malbec

½ cup chicken or vegetable stock

sea salt and freshly ground black pepper

To serve

sautéed potatoes

mixed salad greens

SERVES 4–6

cooking with wine

Large bowls of steaming hot mussels are served in bistros all over France. The classic recipe is *à la marinière*, with shallots and white wine, but here the mussels are cooked in a garlicky, saffron-scented sauce with tomatoes and fennel. If you want to serve this dish as an entrée, the classic accompaniment is French fries.

mussels with fennel, tomatoes, garlic, and saffron

Heat the olive oil in a large sauté pan. Add the onion and fennel and cook until soft, 3–5 minutes. Add the garlic, wine, and tomatoes. Boil for 1 minute, lower the heat, then add the saffron and a pinch of salt. Simmer gently for 15 minutes.

Increase the heat under the sauce and, when boiling, add the prepared mussels. Cover and cook until the mussels open, 2–3 minutes. Discard any that do not open. Serve immediately, sprinkled with parsley.

*Note To prepare mussels, start 15 minutes before you are ready to cook them. Rinse them in cold water and tap any open ones against the work surface. If they don't close, discard them. Scrub the others with a stiff brush and scrape off any barnacles. Pull off and discard the wiry beards.

Recommended wine match The classic match is Muscadet, but Chablis or a (Loire) Sauvignon Blanc would work well, too.

2 tablespoons extra virgin olive oil

1 small onion, chopped

½ fennel bulb, chopped

4 garlic cloves, crushed

1 cup dry white wine

2 cups canned chopped tomatoes, about 16 oz.

a pinch of saffron threads

2 lb. fresh mussels*

coarse sea salt

a handful of flat-leaf parsley, chopped, to serve

SERVES 4

Tuna is a very filling and rich fish. Although one never thinks of cooking it with rosemary, it is a marriage made in heaven, especially when flavored with a dry white wine, good olive oil, and some capers to cut the richness.

tuna steaks baked with rosemary

Coat the tuna steaks with the chopped rosemary. Transfer each steak onto a big square of baking parchment or aluminum foil. Scatter the capers on top, then pour the wine over. Season well with salt and pepper, then drizzle with olive oil. Loosely but securely twist or close the paper or foil around the tuna—it should be loose enough to fill with steam as it cooks, but secure enough not to let the juices escape during the cooking. Bake in a preheated oven at 350°F for 15 minutes. Serve each package on a warmed plate for each diner to open for themselves, with lemon wedges. Garnish with rosemary sprigs, if liked.

Recommended wine match A herby Italian red or white, aromatic Cabernet Franc, or a chunky white like Alsace Pinot Gris.

4 tuna steaks, about 5 oz. each

2 tablespoons chopped fresh rosemary, plus extra sprigs to garnish (optional)

1 tablespoon salted capers, rinsed, dried, and chopped

4 tablespoons dry white wine

4 tablespoons extra virgin olive oil

sea salt and freshly ground black pepper

lemon wedges, to serve

SERVES 4

cooking with wine

This is a really robust pasta dish that's perfect to serve in cold weather. The wine gives a richer, more warming flavor than the usual tomato-based sauce.

rigatoni with eggplant, sausage, and zinfandel sauce

Slit the sausage skins with a sharp knife and remove. Roughly chop the meat. Heat 1 tablespoon olive oil in a large skillet or wok, add the sausage meat, breaking it up with a wooden spoon, and fry until lightly golden. Using a slotted spoon, remove meat from the pan and set aside.

Add 2 more tablespoons oil to the pan, add the eggplant and stir-fry for 3–4 minutes until it starts to brown. Add the remaining oil and the onion and fry for 1–2 minutes, then add the red pepper and fry for 1–2 minutes more. Return the sausage meat to the pan, stir in the tomato paste and cook for 1 minute. Add the garlic, oregano, and wine and simmer until the wine has reduced by half. Stir in the stock and let simmer over low heat for about 10 minutes.

Meanwhile, to cook the pasta, bring a large saucepan of lightly salted water to a boil. Add the pasta and cook for about 10 minutes until *al dente*, or according to the instructions on the package. When the pasta is just cooked, spoon off a couple of tablespoons of the cooking water and stir it into the wine sauce. Drain the pasta thoroughly, then tip it into the sauce. Add 3 tablespoons parsley and mix well. Remove the pan from the heat, cover, and let stand for 2–3 minutes for the flavors to amalgamate.

Add salt and pepper to taste, then spoon into 4 warmed serving bowls. Serve immediately, sprinkled with the remaining parsley.

Recommended wine match A Zinfandel is the obvious choice, but any robust medium- to full-bodied red would work well.

cooking with wine

12 oz. fresh Italian sausages

4 tablespoons olive oil

1 medium eggplant, cut into cubes

1 medium onion, finely chopped

1 red bell pepper, seeded and cut into 1-inch cubes

1 rounded tablespoon tomato paste

2 garlic cloves, crushed

1 teaspoon dried oregano

¾ cup Zinfandel or other full-bodied, fruity red wine

¾ cup fresh chicken stock, or light vegetable stock made from 1 teaspoon vegetable bouillon powder

12 oz. dried pasta tubes, such as rigatoni or penne

4 tablespoons chopped fresh parsley

sea salt and freshly ground black pepper

SERVES 4

A wonderfully light and fragrant risotto, perfect for the summer to serve with cold chicken or fish. Try to use the more fragrant soft herbs here–the more, the merrier.

green herb risotto with white wine and lemon

Put the stock in a saucepan and keep at a gentle simmer. Melt half the butter in a large, heavy saucepan and add the scallions. Cook gently for 3–5 minutes until soft. Pour in the wine, add half the lemon zest, and boil hard until the wine has reduced and almost disappeared. This will remove the taste of raw alcohol. Add the rice, and stir until heated through and well coated with butter and onions.

Begin to add the hot stock, a large ladle at a time, stirring until each ladle has been absorbed by the rice. Continue until the rice is tender and creamy, but the grains still firm. (This should take 15–20 minutes depending on the type of rice used—check the package instructions.)

Taste and season well with salt and lots of freshly ground black pepper. Stir in the remaining butter, the lemon zest, juice, herbs, and Parmesan. Cover and let rest for a couple of minutes, then serve immediately.

Recommended wine match A fragrant white with some freshness: Soave, Sauvignon Blanc, Muscadet, or dry Riesling.

about 1½ quarts vegetable or light chicken stock

4 oz. plus 1 tablespoon unsalted butter

8 scallions, green and white parts, finely chopped

⅔ cup dry white wine

finely grated zest and juice of 1 large unwaxed lemon

2⅓ cups risotto rice

4 tablespoons chopped fresh herbs such as parsley, basil, marjoram, and thyme

⅔ cup freshly grated Parmesan cheese

sea salt and freshly ground black pepper

SERVES 4–6

Poor old celery—it is more often an ingredient than the star of a dish. Braised in wine in this traditional Provençal recipe, however, it takes center stage. Beef is the ideal complement to the trinity of celery, tomatoes, and anchovies, so serve this with roast beef or grilled steaks.

braised celery

Remove any tough outer stalks from the celery and trim the tips so they will just fit into a large sauté pan with a lid.

Bring a large saucepan of water to a boil. Add a pinch of salt, then the celery, and simmer gently for 10 minutes to blanch. Remove, drain, and pat dry with paper towels.

Heat the olive oil in the sauté pan. Add the bacon strips, onion, and carrot and cook gently until lightly browned. Add the celery and a little salt and pepper, and cook just to brown, then remove.

Add the garlic to the pan and cook for 1 minute, then add the tomatoes, wine, and bay leaf. Bring to a boil and cook for 1 minute. Add the celery, then cover and simmer gently for 30 minutes, turning the celery once during cooking.

Transfer the celery to a serving dish. Increase the heat and cook the sauce to reduce it slightly, about 10 minutes. Pour it over the celery, sprinkle with the anchovies and parsley, and serve.

Recommended wine match · On its own, use a mid-weight white— Chardonnay or Viognier. If eating with beef, go red.

2 whole bunches of celery

2 tablespoons extra virgin olive oil

2 thick slices of bacon, cut into thin strips

1 onion, halved, then quartered and sliced

1 carrot, halved lengthwise, then quartered and sliced

2 garlic cloves, sliced

1 cup canned chopped tomatoes, about 8 oz.

1 cup dry white wine

1 fresh bay leaf

8 anchovies, chopped

a handful of flat-leaf parsley, chopped

coarse sea salt and freshly ground black pepper

SERVES 4–6

cooking with wine

Baking sliced potatoes with mushrooms in layers allows the potatoes to absorb the wine and the earthy flavor of the mushrooms. Try to use the darkest mushrooms you can for this, as they will have the best taste—you can always mix fresh with reconstituted dried mushrooms, such as porcini, for a more intense flavor.

potatoes baked with wine and mushrooms

Peel the potatoes and slice thickly, adding them to a bowl of cold water as you go. Trim and slice the mushrooms thickly. Heat the olive oil in a large skillet and add the mushrooms and garlic. Fry for about 5 minutes until beginning to brown. Stir in the parsley. Put a layer of half the potatoes in the bottom of a deep gratin dish, drizzle with olive oil, and cover this with a layer of half the mushrooms, seasoning as you go.* Cover with a layer of the remaining potatoes, drizzle with olive oil, then add a layer of the remaining mushrooms and drizzle with oil. Pour in the wine, cover with aluminum foil and bake in a preheated oven at 350°F for 30 minutes. Uncover and cook for a further 30 minutes or until the potatoes are completely tender.

*Note To halve the cooking time, blanch the sliced potatoes in boiling salted water for 5 minutes before layering up.

Recommended wine match A good, slightly older white Burgundy would be perfect here.

2 lb. medium-size potatoes

1½ lb. flavorsome mushrooms, such as dark flat cap, chestnut, or portobello field mushrooms (or fresh wild mushrooms if you can find them)

¾ cup extra virgin olive oil, plus extra for drizzling

2 garlic cloves, finely chopped

¼ cup chopped fresh parsley

⅓ cup dry white wine or vermouth

sea salt and freshly ground black pepper

a deep gratin dish

SERVES 4

This simple but delicious combination is a refreshingly light way to round off an otherwise quite rich menu. If champagne seems a bit decadent, use a good bottle of cava or an American sparkling wine.

raspberries in champagne gelatin

Put 3 tablespoons hot water into a small bowl and sprinkle in the gelatin. Set aside in a warm place to dissolve, for about 10 minutes. Divide the raspberries between the glasses. Open the champagne and add a little to the dissolved gelatin. Transfer to a pitcher and add the remaining champagne. Mix gently so that you don't build up a froth. Pour into the glasses on top of the raspberries and chill for 2 hours, until set.

Recommended wine match Tricky, but an off-dry rosé champagne is your best bet, or perhaps a late-harvest Alsace Pinot Gris.

2 envelopes powdered gelatin, ½ oz. each, or 2 tablespoons

1 lb. raspberries, about 3 cups

1 bottle champagne, at room temperature

8 glasses

SERVES 8

Roasting pears in wine transforms them from everyday fruit into a light but luxurious dinner-party dessert. Their gentle flavor makes a perfect foil for a fine dessert wine. The trick is to use an inexpensive wine for cooking and a better wine of the same type to serve with it.

roasted pears with sweet wine, honey, and pine nuts

Strain the lemon juice into a small bowl. Cut the pears in half, peel them, and remove the cores. Dip the pear halves in the lemon juice (this will prevent them discoloring), then put them, cut sides upwards, in the prepared ovenproof dish. Make sure the pears fit snugly in one layer. Put a small knob of butter in the hollow of each pear, then drizzle them with the honey, wine, and any remaining lemon juice.

Bake in a preheated oven at 375°F for 50–60 minutes, turning the pears over halfway through. If the pears are producing a lot of juice while they are cooking, increase the oven temperature to 400°F to concentrate the juices and form a syrup. Remove the pears from the oven and let cool for about 20 minutes.

Meanwhile, lightly toast the pine nuts in a dry, nonstick skillet, shaking the pan occasionally, until they start to brown. Sprinkle over the sugar and continue to cook until the sugar melts and caramelizes. Put the cream and vanilla sugar in a small saucepan and heat gently, stirring occasionally, until lukewarm.

To serve, put 3 pear halves on each plate, trickle over 1 tablespoon warm cream and scatter over a few caramelized pine nuts. Alternatively, serve the cream separately for your guests to pour over.

Recommended wine match This is a good dessert to pair with a Sauternes or another sweet Bordeaux-style wine.

freshly squeezed juice of
1 large lemon

9 medium just-ripe Anjou pears

4 tablespoons butter, softened

3 tablespoons clear fragrant honey, such as orange blossom

¾ cup Premières Côtes de Bordeaux or a late-harvested Sauvignon or Sémillon

⅓ cup pine nuts

2 teaspoons sugar

¾ cup heavy cream

2 teaspoons vanilla sugar or ½ teaspoon pure vanilla extract mixed with 2 teaspoons sugar

a large ovenproof dish, buttered (large enough to take the pears in a single layer)

SERVES 6

This trifle is just delicious but, instead of custard, it is made using a mixture of cream and mascarpone. Go to an Italian delicatessen for Vin Santo (a sweet wine) and biscotti (hard, almond-flavored Italian biscuits). These are traditionally eaten dipped into the wine, but here make a splendid addition to trifle.

vin santo trifle

Put the biscotti into a large serving bowl, preferably glass. Pour over the Vin Santo and arrange the figs and cherries on top. Put the cream into a bowl and whip lightly until soft peaks form. Add the mascarpone and sugar and continue beating until stiff. Spoon the cream and mascarpone mixture over the fruit, then sprinkle with almonds. Using a vegetable peeler (or an Italian truffle slicer if you have one), make curls with the white chocolate and sprinkle over the trifle. Chill until required.

Recommended wine match This trifle cries out for an indulgent glass of Madeira.

8 oz. Italian biscotti

½ cup Vin Santo

8 ripe figs, quartered lengthwise

1 can pitted cherries, 15 oz.

2 cups heavy cream

1 lb. mascarpone cheese

⅓ cup sugar

½ cup slivered almonds

2 squares white chocolate, 2 oz.

SERVES 8

There is nothing quite as sensual as warm zabaglione served straight from the pan. Many like to beat it in a copper bowl so that it cooks quickly. The secret is not to let the mixture get too hot, but still hot enough to cook and thicken the egg yolks. The proportions are easy to remember: one egg yolk to one tablespoon sugar to one tablespoon Marsala serves one person. It must be made at the last moment, but it doesn't take long and is well worth the effort.

zabaglione

Put the egg yolks, Marsala, and sugar in a medium heatproof bowl (preferably copper or stainless steel) and beat with a hand-held electric mixer or a wire whisk until well blended.

Set the bowl over a saucepan of gently simmering water—the bottom should at no time be in contact with the water. Do not let the water boil. Beat the mixture until it is glossy, pale, light, and fluffy and holds a trail when dropped from the whisk. This should take about 5 minutes. Serve immediately in warmed cocktail glasses with ladyfingers for dipping.

Variation To make chilled zabaglione for two, when cooked, remove the bowl from the heat and beat until completely cold. In a separate bowl, beat ⅔ cup heavy cream until floppy, then fold into the cold zabaglione. Spoon into glasses and chill for 2–3 hours.

Recommended wine match Go traditional and serve it with what you put in it, Marsala, or a sweet Maderia.

2 large egg yolks

2 tablespoons sweet Marsala wine

2 tablespoons sugar

savoiardi or ladyfingers, for dipping

SERVES 2

cooking with wine

Wine and fruit make fabulously pretty fruit jellies that offer a refreshing end to a dinner party.
You don't have to use a sweet wine for these; just add sugar syrup to taste.

sparkling shiraz
and summer berry jellies

Put the gelatin in a flat dish and sprinkle over 3 tablespoons cold water. Let soak for 3 minutes until soft, then drain off the water. Heat the sparkling wine in a saucepan until hot but not boiling. Tip the soaked gelatin into the wine and stir until dissolved. Set aside and let cool.

Rinse the berries, then put them in a shallow bowl. Cut the strawberries in half or quarters, depending on their size. Sprinkle over the sugar and set aside to macerate.

Check the liquid jelly for sweetness and add sugar syrup to taste. Put an assortment of berries in the bottom of 6 glasses or glass dishes and pour over enough jelly to cover them. Put the jellies in the refrigerator and let set, 45–60 minutes. Add the remaining fruit to the glasses and top with the remaining jelly. (If the jelly in the saucepan has started to set, reheat it very gently, stirring, until smooth and liquid, then let cool before pouring it over the fruit.) Return the jellies to the refrigerator for another 45–60 minutes, until set. Serve with cream or vanilla ice cream.

*Note To make the sugar syrup, put ½ cup sugar and ⅔ cup water in a saucepan and heat gently until the sugar has dissolved. Bring to a boil and simmer for 3–4 minutes. You can use the syrup immediately, or let it cool and store it in the refrigerator for up to 2 weeks.

Recommended wine match A chilled ruby port or, if it's hot outside, an off-dry sparkler—maybe a Moscato d'Asti.

4 sheets of leaf gelatin or 1 package powdered gelatin

2¼ cups sparkling Shiraz or other sparkling red wine

2⅔ cups mixed berries, such as strawberries, raspberries, blackberries, or blueberries

1–2 tablespoons sugar

3–4 tablespoons sugar syrup*

cream or vanilla ice cream, to serve

6 individual glass dishes

SERVES 6

cooking with wine

Combining chocolate with a strong red wine like Cabernet Sauvignon might sound like an unlikely idea, but if you think about the wine's red berry flavors it makes sense. It also adds an intriguing edge to this dessert that will keep your guests guessing. The ideal Cabernet to use is one that is ripe and fruity but not too oaky.

chocolate and cabernet pots

Put the wine and sugar in a saucepan and heat gently until the sugar has dissolved. Increase the heat very slightly and simmer gently until the wine has reduced by two-thirds to about 4 tablespoons, 20–25 minutes.

Meanwhile, break the chocolate into squares, and put them in a blender. Blitz briefly to break them into small pieces.

Put the cream in a saucepan and heat until almost boiling. Pour the hot cream over the chocolate in the blender, then add the hot, sweetened wine. Leave for a few seconds so the chocolate melts. Whizz briefly until the mixture is smooth. Add the egg and cinnamon and whizz again briefly to mix.

Pour the mixture into 6 or 8 ramekins or espresso cups, then chill in the refrigerator for 3–4 hours. Remove the chocolate pots from the refrigerator 20 minutes before serving. To serve, sprinkle a thin layer of cocoa powder over the top of each pot, then sprinkle with a little sifted confectioners' sugar, if liked.

Recommended wine match A small glass of vintage character or late-bottled vintage port would work well with these chocolate pots.

¾ cup fruity Cabernet Sauvignon, preferably from California, Chile, or Australia

2 tablespoons sugar

7 oz. plain dark chocolate (70% cocoa solids)

1¼ cups light cream

1 egg

a pinch of ground cinnamon

To serve

2 teaspoons cocoa

confectioners' sugar (optional)

6 or 8 small pots, ramekins, or espresso coffee cups, ½ cup each

SERVES 6–8

WINE
practicalities

Learning how to taste wine will give you more enjoyment from every glass. This chapter tells you how to run a fun tasting at home, and how to store and serve your wine well.

People tend to get embarrassed about tasting wine **properly**. But there's a good reason for all the swirling, **sniffing**, and spitting: to bring as many of your senses into play in **assessing** the wine as you can.

tasting wine

However, the spitting is only necessary if you're tasting a whole stack of wines; there's no need to do it at the dinner table! There are a couple of things here that make a big difference to any tasting. Number one: Get a decent-sized glass that will allow you to swirl the wine around a lot (see page 230). Number two: Make sure the wine is at the right temperature (see page 229).

Next, you're onto tasting. There's no great mystique to this. In fact, it's quite easy to get the hang of, once you realize that tasters' notes tend to follow a set pattern, analyzing the different elements of the wine (see opposite and Setting up a tasting at home on page 218). There's a tasting notes template that you can photocopy on page 224.

What does it look like?

Fill your glass about a third of the way, and look at the color. Tilting it against a white background helps. For whites, if it's pale, it's still young; if it's a darker yellow, it may well have some age on it. For reds, bright vibrant ruby means a youthful wine. If it's got browner hues, it's aging. (If a wine is cloudy, it's faulty.) Want to get an early indicator of the alcohol level? Swirl it and watch the "tears" roll down the side of the glass. Big thick ones mean a higher alcohol content.

What does it smell like?

Swirl the wine around a bit (now you see why you need a big glass) and take a good sniff. The wine should smell of fruit, not grapes. Take a look at the flavor table on page 225 for typical aromas, but the main thing is to go with your instincts. If you think a wine smells of old car tires or chocolate cake, say so!

What does it taste like?

Take a sip and sloosh it around your mouth. This isn't so much about flavor, interestingly, but the structure of the wine. Remember, tasting is totally subjective; there are no right or wrong answers. Think about the following. (There are good tests for tannin, alcohol, and acidity on page 224 under Structure.)

• Is it full-flavored or not? What does it taste of? See page 225 for ideas.

• How high are the tannins (in red wines) and the acidity level (in reds and whites)?

• Is it sweet or dry?

• Does it have high levels of alcohol?

• How full-bodied is it? Is it in balance? A wine's "body," incidentally, means how much weight it carries in your mouth. If you scored water as 0 and molasses as 100, wines should come in between 20 (the lightest) and 70.

Anyone who has even a passing interest in wine should do this. It's a cheap night, generates debate, and introduces people to new wines. The beauty of a tasting is that it's far easier to compare and contrast two wines that are sitting next to each other than trying to remember whether you prefer Wine X in your glass to the one you tasted last week.

setting up a tasting at home

How many wines should I put on?

Volume-wise, I would reckon on about a bottle per person, with a maximum of ten wines to try. Most people can't taste more than ten at one go because either they get bored or their palate gets tired. Better to taste half a dozen interesting wines with everyone paying attention than slog through 20 duller bottles.

Which wines should I choose?

It helps to have some sort of a theme and also a bit of variation. While wines picked at random are OK, it's more interesting if people are asked to draw a conclusion at the end of the night.

Themes might be: ten wines from one retailer at a variety of prices; Old World versus New World; French reds and whites; best wines on discount that week; California Cabernet versus French or Australian; best grape varietal without food; unusual styles or countries. The list is endless—just target it to the interest range (and budget) of your friends.

The variation aspect is important, because not many people want to taste ten very similar wines. Indeed, the joy of a social tasting is that you can throw in wine styles that aren't drunk all that often to see if people like them: port, sherry, amarone, dessert wine, German Riesling. It's always worth putting one in to see what people think.

What price wines should I choose?

This depends a bit on the level of expertise of your friends, but for the most part I'd suggest a spread, finishing with at least one pricey wine of the sort that people don't often buy. Charging people to come along is a good idea; that way, if your guests want cheap or expensive wines, they can pay accordingly, and you're not out of pocket. If you have charged six friends $20 each to come, you could buy two wines at $15, one each at $20 and $30 and one at $40. The point is to give people the chance to find wines that they like, and also to broaden their tasting education.

WHAT YOU NEED ON THE NIGHT

• A corkscrew. Obviously!

• Plenty of the right sort of glasses (see page 230), and at least two per person, so people can compare different wines. Wine merchants often rent them if you don't have enough.

• A bucket for people to spit or tip their wine into.

• Pens and paper for people to write down their scores.

• Plastic bags or brown paper and rubber bands, with which to cover up the wine bottles. This means that any tasting is done "blind" and stops people's prejudices from getting in the way. It's also a lot of fun trying to guess the grape variety and where a wine is from.

WHAT TO PREPARE IN ADVANCE

• Make sure that all the wines are at the right temperature (see page 229). If your room is warm and the bottles are going to be out for a while, you might want a bowl or bucket full of ice for some of the whites.

• Open the wines and bag them all beforehand so you're not wrestling with corks and rubber bands when you should be tasting. Make sure you number each bag and keep a note of which is which.

• Flight the wines in this order: fizzy, white, red, sweet white, fortified. Within that, taste the lightest wines first and the heaviest last. For whites, the tasting order would be roughly Riesling, Sauvignon Blanc, Chenin Blanc, Viognier, Sémillon, Chardonnay. Reds would be Beaujolais, Barbera, Valpolicella, Cabernet Franc, Tempranillo/Rioja, Malbec, Pinotage, Grenache, Merlot, Cabernet Sauvignon, Syrah/Shiraz, Zinfandel. If you're sampling two or more wines of the same varietal, taste the cheapest first.

Don't feel you have to write lengthy tasting notes.
The point is to think about what's in your glass
rather than glugging it uncritically, and to have fun.

RUNNING THE TASTING

Explain to people what the point of the tasting is. Pour samples of the first wine and get everyone to sniff it together. Throw the floor open to the following questions as you work through the tasting notes template on page 224:

- Is it light or dark in color?
- Is it strongly aromatic or not?
- Does it smell of anything in particular? Fruit? Oak?
- Does anyone have any ideas what it might be?

Then let them taste it and answer the questions on page 217 (What does it taste like?).

Then it's conclusions time.
- Did people like it? Get them to score it out of ten.
- What's the finish like—for how long after you've spat or swallowed the wine can you still taste it?
- How much do people think it cost?
- Is it ready to drink or does it need more time?
- When might they drink it? On its own? With food? If so, what type of food?
- Does anyone have any idea what it might be now?

Don't feel you have to write lengthy tasting notes. The description "Soft, fruity, nice on its own, 7/10" is fine, as is "Smelled like my grandmother's cat—zero." The point is to think about what's in your glass rather than glugging it uncritically, to have fun, and to make some exciting discoveries. If you have regular tastings, you could keep a list of the top-scoring wines and have a "champion of champions" tasting once a year.

If you're stuck for what you should be looking for in a wine, the following pointers might help you. See page 217 for extra help.

tasting notes template

APPEARANCE

- Clear or hazy?
- Bubbles in sparkling wine: fine or fat, fast or slow?
- "Legs" ("tears" down the side of the glass): these are an indicator of alcohol. The thicker the tears, the stronger the wine.
- Color: whites—pale (green tints), lemon, golden; rosé: pale pink, bright pink, orange; reds—purple, ruby, garnet, brick-colored, tawny.

NOSE

- Does it smell faulty? (See pages 232–233.)
- What flavors can you pick out? (See opposite.)
- How intense is it?

PALATE

- What flavors do you find in your mouth? (See opposite.)

STRUCTURE

- How high are the tannins? Tannin is felt on the gums and teeth, and is an essential component of red wines. Once you've spat, run your tongue around your teeth; if they feel dry, that's tannin. Red wines need enough to hold them together, but not so much as to rip the enamel off your molars.

- How high is the acidity? Acidity is detected down the sides of the mouth. Imagine sucking a lemon—that's acidity. If you're among friends, you can do the "dribble test." Once you've spat or swallowed the wine, open your mouth and tilt your head down. If you start to drool, that's acidity. All wines (even reds) need a little acidity to stop them from being flabby.
- How high is the alcohol level? This essential component shouldn't really be noticeable. If a wine finishes "hot" on the back of your throat, it's got too much alcohol for its weight.
- Is it sweet or dry?
- Body (weight): does it feel "big" or "small" in the mouth?
- Do the flavor and the structure seem balanced, or is there more of one than the other?

FINISH

- How long does the wine's flavor stay with you once you've spat it out or swallowed it?

CONCLUSIONS

- Did you like it?
- How much would you pay for it?
- Is it ready for drinking now?
- When, and with what food, would you drink it?

Most wines don't smell of grapes, but of a variety of fruit flavors, **vegetation**, savory or **floral** scents. The table below will help you pinpoint exactly what it is you're smelling in the wines—if it smells **citrussy**, for example, try to narrow this down to a particular fruit.

key flavors

NUTTY	Almonds, coconuts, hazelnuts, walnuts
FLORAL	Blossom, elderflower, honeysuckle, lime leaf, jasmine, roses, violets
VEGETAL/ HERBAL	Grass (fresh), hay, fennel, nettles, privet, mint/menthol, eucalyptus, green pepper, tomato
CITRUS FRUIT	Apples, pears, lemons, grapefruit, limes, mandarins
EXOTIC FRUIT	Gooseberries, grapes, melons, litchis, bananas, mangoes
STONE FRUIT	Nectarines, peaches, apricots
DARK FRUIT	Plums, damsons, blackcurrants, prunes
SUMMER FRUIT	Raspberries, strawberries, redcurrants, loganberries, morello cherries, blueberries, blackberries, black cherries
SWEET	Turkish delight, barley sugar, butterscotch, honey, toffee, raisins, chocolate, molasses
SPICES	Brioche/toast, cookies, vanilla, cinnamon, cloves, black/white pepper, tea, incense, tobacco, licorice
SAVORY	Earth, farmyard, truffles, kerosene, minerals, gunpowder, smoke, tar, black olives, coffee, wax, cedar, pencil lead
FAULTY	Wet cardboard, vinegary, oxidized

storing

When it comes to drinking at home, **buying** the right wine in the first place is only part of achieving **vinous nirvana**; you need to treat your new purchase right if you're to get the most out of it.

If you're planning to drink a wine within a week of purchase, it doesn't really matter where you keep it. Any longer, and it helps to bear the following in mind. You'll save yourself a lot of ruined bottles.

WHERE TO STORE IT

Wine likes the sort of conditions that humans don't: cool, humid, and dark. The ideal temperature is about 50°F (10°C). If you have a cellar, perfect. If not, find a place that fulfills as many criteria as possible. But (and it's a big but) bear in mind that big temperature swings are an absolute no-no, so storing it in the garage is out. Better to find somewhere that's dark and a bit too warm but constant—maybe a hallway or under the stairs where it's a steady 60°F (15°C)—than somewhere the temperature fluctuates wildly.

HOW TO STORE IT

In a word: horizontally. The lapping of the wine stops the cork from drying out.

HOW LONG TO STORE IT FOR

This depends on two things: the environment and the wine itself. The warmer it is, the faster a wine ages, so a bottle that might last a couple of years in a cellar will probably be shot after six months in your living room. Then there's the question of whether your wine will improve with age, even if it's well kept. Some fine wines will age for decades. Most modern wines (reds and whites) are ready to drink immediately and are likely to deteriorate, rather than improve, with time. So if in doubt, pull the cork!

Serving wine correctly is easy–and doing it well can have a big impact on what it tastes like. Two things, plus getting the right glass (see over), are key to making the most of your bottle.

serving

TEMPERATURE

There's a tendency to overchill whites and serve reds too warm. This is bad news. White wine that's too cold loses all its flavors, while a too-hot red wine tastes unbalanced, and its alcohol is exaggerated.

Red wines should be served at room temperature, but as the notion of "reds at room temperature" was established long before the advent of central heating, you might want to leave your bottles in a cooler part of the house (or even outside) before bringing them to the table. This is particularly important if you keep your house like a sauna! 61–64°F (16–18°C) is a good temperature for reds.

Whites need to be cool, but not too cold, so if your fridge is particularly ferocious (and most fridges are colder than the ideal white wine temperature), take wines out half an hour or so before serving them.

DECANTING

Most reds, and even some whites, are improved by decanting, since it gets oxygen into the wine and opens up its flavors. Decant reds several hours beforehand. Whites can be done just before serving. To decant a bottle of wine, leave the bottle to stand upright for a couple of hours to settle, then pour it ever so slowly into a decanter (or jug if you don't have one) a few hours before serving. If you carry out this process over a candle or a light, you'll see the sediment start to gather at the shoulder of the bottle. When it's about to come over the shoulder and down the bottle's neck, stop. (If you're decanting port, there'll probably be half an inch left in the bottle.)

Getting the correct glass is the last thing you have to get right before actually drinking the stuff, and, even though it's often overlooked, in some ways it's the most important factor of all. After all, to an extent you can get away with a wine that's a bit too warm or a bit too cold, but there's not much you can do if your glass is killing the aromas.

Hyperbolic nonsense, you might think; surely a glass is a glass is a glass? But you'd be wrong. The shape and size of your wine glass have a big bearing on how your wine actually tastes. Fortunately, there are only two basic rules. First, within reason, the bigger, the better. And second, the glass should be wider at the bottom and tapered toward the top in a kind of closed tulip shape. Professional tasters use what are known as ISO glasses, and if you can get them, they're great for tastings or during the week (you might want something fancier for weekends).

Fancier, incidentally, shouldn't mean cripplingly expensive. Plenty of crystalware manufacturers sell hugely expensive, ornately carved creations that are considerably more effective as a decoration than as a means of serving wine. So don't, for goodness sake, buy something expensive and fancy-looking if it is small or has straight sides.

So, you want explanations? OK, here we go. The beauty of a large glass is that you can fill it only a third of the way, which allows you to give the wine a good swirl, releasing the wine's aromas and increasing the taste experience. Small glasses, full to the brim, rob you of that opportunity, as, indeed, do glasses with a straight edge, since the wine tends to fly out of the top. Irrespective of the fact that you won't have to replace your carpet every year, there's another reason why a tapered glass works better: it concentrates the flavors that you've generated with your swirling by funneling them to a point.

Companies like Schott and Riedel have built entire collections of different-shaped glasses, all designed to show off the characteristics of different styles of wine. However, unless you have unlimited storage space and deep pockets, one set of glasses for wine, a set of flutes for champagne, and some ISO glasses for port, sherry, and even hard liquor will be fine.

If I had a **dollar bill** for every time somebody served me good wine, at the perfect temperature, but in a bloody **awful** glass, and I've been **underwhelmed** by the experience as a result, I'd be able to buy myself a fair few cases.

wine glasses

wine faults

Wine is a living product, which is what makes it interesting. But it also means that things can go wrong, affecting the taste of what's in your glass. Being able to spot these faults is important; you don't want to drink a bad bottle just because you didn't realize it was off.

CORKED

The most common wine fault, cork taint happens when the cork is infected with a smelly mold, which then transfers its aroma to the bottle. High levels of cork taint are quite distinctive, giving a grotty smell of wet cardboard and old socks. Lower levels are much harder to spot. Chances are, the wine will just taste a bit low on fruit and you won't like it much. Current estimates put cork taint in wine at about 5%—quite high. The only way to avoid it is to buy bottles with plastic stoppers or screw caps. More and more wines (particularly New World whites) have these closures.

OXIDIZED

Contact with air is an integral part of making some wines (Madeira and tawny port, for instance), but for the overwhelming majority it's a no-no. It turns red wines brown, white wines dark yellow, and knocks the freshness out of both. If your wine looks odd and tastes tired and dull, it may well be oxidized.

VINEGARY

Poor hygiene in the winery can lead to acetic acid in the wine. If you leave a bottle of wine open for a couple of days, then drink it, you'll get the same effect—so try it, remember it, and don't tolerate it.

CLOUDY

A wine that is cloudy is definitely faulty, since this means it contains yeast and bacteria. Don't confuse cloudiness (bad) with sediment, often found in top-end wines that haven't been filtered in the winery.

FIZZY

Still wine should be just that—still. If it's fizzy, it means that it has undergone an unintended secondary fermentation in the bottle and should be replaced.

COOKED

Wine needs cool storage. If, on its journey from vineyard to outlet, it's been left in the sun or a warm warehouse, the wine can start to "cook." Fruit flavors will be baked and tired, not fresh and vibrant, as a result. It's intentional in Madeira, but nowhere else.

SULFURY

Nearly every winery uses sulfur dioxide in the winemaking process to help preserve its wine. If they get a bit heavy-handed, the wine will smell of struck matches or rubber. Sometimes you can make it go away by swirling the wine around a bit.

TAKING A BOTTLE BACK

If you think a wine is faulty, it should be replaced. Stores are not allowed to sell goods that are below merchantable quality, and must replace defective items. If your wine is faulty, take it back as soon as you can so it doesn't have time to get vinegary. It's a good idea to phone first. You will be viewed more sympathetically if you haven't drunk most of the bottle!

In a restaurant, the waiter should pour you a sample to try before pouring the rest. If you have concerns, raise them then. Even if he thinks the wine is all right, you can still reasonably request that it be replaced; that's why they pour you a sample.

wine words

ACIDITY
An essential element of whites and (to a lesser extent) red wines, adding freshness.

APPELLATION
A region that defines the limits of where it's possible to produce a particular style of wine. Bordeaux, Chianti, Champagne, Napa Valley, and Burgundy are all appellations.

BALANCE
The way a wine's fruit flavors, structure, and alcohol levels interact. If one of these dominates, a wine is out of balance.

BARRIQUE
French for "barrel," but adopted all over the world. Used for aging and fermenting wine.

BLUSH WINE
Pale pink wine made of red grapes (often sweet).

BODY
The "size" of a wine in the mouth—the flavor and weight it has.

BOTRYTIS
Mold that develops on grapes in sweet-wine areas, causing them to shrivel and concentrate their flavors. Also called noble rot.

BOUQUET
Wine's aroma. (Good wines have plenty of it!)

CAPE BLEND
A South African red, a mix of "international" varietals like Cabernet and/or Merlot with the local varietal, Pinotage.

CLARET
Red Bordeaux. Some use the name to mean generic red wine.

CORK TAINT/CORKED
See page 233.

CRU
French word meaning "growth," but usually referring to a specific vineyard. The *Premiers Crus* (first growths) of the Médoc, for instance, are that region's most hallowed wine estates, such as Château Latour. *Grand Cru* is the top Burgundy designation.

CRUSH
The grape harvest.

CUVÉE
French word (again) meaning a blend of different wines.

D.O.
A Spanish appellation: *Denominación de Origen*.

DRY
A wine that has no sugar left in it.

EISWEIN
Super-sweet wine made from grapes picked so late there's snow and ice on the berries.

ESTATE-BOTTLED
Wine bottled at the same place that it was made. *Mis en bouteille au château* in French.

FERMENTATION
The process that turns sugar (in grapes) into alcohol. The more sugar there is in a grape when it's picked, the higher the potential alcohol.

FINISH
The intensity of flavors left in your mouth once you've swallowed the wine. Some finishes can last for minutes.

GRAPE VARIETAL OR GRAPE VARIETY
The type of grape used to make the wine, e.g. Cabernet Sauvignon.

GREEN
An under-ripe wine.

ICE WINE
See Eiswein.

LBV
Late-bottled vintage, a type of port.

MACERATION
The process by which fermenting grape juice is left sitting on its skins. Used to add color and tannin to red wines.

MAGNUM
A 1.5-liter bottle (double normal size). Also a mustachioed private eye.

MERITAGE
American name for a red wine made with a blend of the classic Bordeaux grapes, Cabernet Sauvignon, Merlot, and Cabernet Franc (plus, sometimes, Petit Verdot).

NEW WORLD
Wine-producing countries outside Europe: Argentina, Chile, Australia, New Zealand, South Africa, and the United States.

NOSE
A wine's smell. Also used as a verb.

OAK
Wines often spend time in oak barrels, which adds a spicy, toasty, or vanilla flavor.

OLD WORLD
The European wine-producing countries.

RESIDUAL SUGAR
The amount of sugar left in a wine once the fermentation is finished. Wine with high residual sugar will taste sweet.

ROSÉ
Pink wine made from red grapes.

SECONDARY FERMENTATION
Puts bubbles in the wine. An integral part of champagne production, but a fault in still wines.

STRUCTURE
Tannin and acidity; the skeleton on which a wine's fruit flavors hang. Without them, it tastes like grape juice.

SUPERTUSCAN
A top-class wine made in the Chianti region, but using large amounts of Cabernet Sauvignon.

TANNIN
An essential component of red wines, providing structure (see above). If your teeth feel dry once you've swallowed, that's tannin.

TAWNY
A pale orangy/brown color that gives its name to a style of port.

TERROIR
French word meaning the combination of geography, climate, and soil that makes a place's wines taste as they do.

ULLAGE
Gap between the surface of the wine in a bottle and the bottom of the cork.

VACUVIN
A useful vacuum system for keeping wine fresh.

VINICULTURE
The science of turning grapes into wine (vinifying them).

VITICULTURE
The science of growing grapes.

YIELD
The number of grapes produced in any area. A low yield gives grapes with a greater flavor concentration.

wine practicalities

index

Main references are in **bold**.

picture credits

Key: **ph**=photographer, **a**=above, **b**=below, **r**=right, **l**=left, **c**=center.   All photographs by Alan Williams unless otherwise stated.

Front endpaper right ph Peter Cassidy; **page 6b** Berry Brothers & Rudd Ltd, London (www.bbr.com); **11ar** Maison M. Chapoutier, Châteauneuf-du-Pape, France (www.chapoutier.com); **12** Viña Errázuriz, Don Maximiano Estate, Aconcagua Valley, Chile (www.errazuriz.cl); **16** Jordan Vineyard & Winery of Sonoma County, California (www.jordanwinery.com); **26ar & cr** Bouchard Père et Fils, Grands Vin de Bourgogne, France (www.bouchard-pereetfils.com); **26br inset** Champagne Ruinart, Reims, France—plus ancienne maison de champagne (www.ruinart.com); **27 inset & 29** William Fèvre, Grands Vin de Chablis, France (www.williamfevre.com); **33bl & ar** Maison M. Chapoutier, Tain l'Hermitage, France; **33br** Châteauneuf-du-Pape, France; **34l** Maison Trimbach in Ribeauvillé, Alsace, France (www.maison-trimbach.fr); **35a ph** David Munns; **36cr** Scrimaglio Winery, Italy (www.scrimaglio.it); **40r ph** Francesca Yorke; **40al & 41al ph** Kurt Mayer © courtesy of Weinbau-Domäne Schloss Johannisberg (www.schloss-johannisberg.com); **41ar** © courtesy of Weinbau-Domäne Schloss Johannisberg; **42al ph** Rui Cunha © courtesy of Symington Family Estates, Portugal (www.symington.com); **42cr&br ph** Miguel Potes © courtesy of Symington Family Estates, Portugal; **42ar, bl, & bc** © courtesy of Nyetimber Vineyard, England (www.nyetimber-vineyard.com); **44al & ar** Jordan Vineyard & Winery of Sonoma County, California; **46a** Jordan Vineyard & Winery of Sonoma County, California; **46b** Ridge Vineyards, Santa Cruz Mountains, California (www.ridgewine.com); **49a** Chateau Montelena Winery, Napa Valley, California (www.montelena.com); **50al** Viña Errázuriz, Aconcagua Valley, Chile; **50–51b** Viña Errázuriz, Don Maximiano Estate, Aconcagua Valley, Chile; Viña Concha y Toro, Casablanca Valley, Chile (www.conchaytoro.com); **52al, ar, & 52–53b ph** Alain Proust © courtesy of Wines of South Africa (www.wosa.co.za); **52cr** © Franz-Marc Frei/Corbis; **53l inset ph** Sven Lennert © courtesy of Wines of South Africa; **53r inset ph** Aline Balayer © courtesy of Wines of South Africa; **58al** © courtesy of Allied Domecq Wines (NZ) Ltd/New Zealand Winegrowers (www.adwnz.com/www.nzwine.com); **58br** © courtesy of Nobilo Wine Group Ltd/New Zealand Winegrowers (www.nobilo.co.nz); **58ar & 59l** © courtesy of Craggy Range Vineyards/New Zealand Winegrowers (www.craggyrange.com); **59r ph** Francesca Yorke; **61cr ph** Francesca Yorke; **62bl** Chateau Montelena Winery, Napa Valley, California; **67al & bl** Azienda Agricola Maculan, Breganze (www.maculan.net); **73l** Maison M. Chapoutier, Tain l'Hermitage; **75bl ph** Francesca Yorke; **79a** Castello D'Abola, Radda in Chianti, Tuscany, Italy (www.albola.com); **87b** Viña Concha y Toro, Maipo Valley, Chile; **90 ph** Francesca Yorke; **96r & inset center ph** Francesca Yorke; **103b both** Chateau Montelena Winery, Napa Valley, California; **104 ph** Francesca Yorke; **110b ph** Francesca Yorke; **111b** William Fèvre, Grands Vin de Chablis, France; **112ar ph** Francesca Yorke; **114 ph** Peter Cassidy; **115 ph** Francesca Yorke; **117** Peter Cassidy; **118al** Peter Cassidy; **120–121 background ph** Peter Cassidy; **121ac & b** Champagne Ruinart, Reims, France—plus ancienne maison de champagne; **123l** Maison M. Chapoutier, Tain l'Hermitage, France; **126 & 128ar ph** William Lingwood; **130, 131l, & 131r ph** Francesca Yorke; **131cl & cr ph** Peter Cassidy; **132a ph** Peter Cassidy; **133 ph** Debi Treloar; **137l & ar ph** Ian Wallace; **138ar & b ph** Debi Treloar; **140l ph** Francesca Yorke; **140–141 ph** Debi Treloar; **144 &145r ph** Debi Treloar; **145l ph** Peter Cassidy; **146 ph** Debi Treloar; **147l ph** Peter Cassidy; **149 both ph** Francesca Yorke; **151 main ph** Debi Treloar; **151 inset ph** Peter Cassidy; **153br ph** Francesca Yorke; **155bl ph** Ian Wallace; **156 & 157cr ph** Debi Treloar; **157l ph** Peter Cassidy; **158ar & 158bl ph** Francesca Yorke; **160r & 161l ph** Martin Brigdale; **161r ph** Francesca Yorke; **162 & 163l ph** Peter Cassidy; **164 ph** Francesca Yorke; **165 ph** Diana Miller; **167b, 168a inset, & 168–169b inset ph** Peter Cassidy; **170a ph** Ian Wallace; **170b ph** Martin Brigdale; **171 ph** Peter Cassidy; **172 ph** Martin Brigdale; **173l & cl ph** Peter Cassidy; **173cr ph** William Lingwood; **173r ph** Debi Treloar; **174 ph** Peter Cassidy; **177 ph** Debi Treloar; **178 & 181 ph** Peter Cassidy; **182 & 185 ph** William Lingwood; **186 ph** Martin Brigdale; **189 ph** William Lingwood; **190 ph** Martin Brigdale; **193 ph** Peter Cassidy; **194 ph** William Lingwood; **197 & 198 ph** Martin Brigdale; **201 ph** Peter Cassidy; **202 ph** Debi Treloar; **205 ph** William Lingwood; **206 ph** Debi Treloar; **209 ph** Martin Brigdale; **210 & 213 ph** William Lingwood; **214 ph** Peter Cassidy; **215l & cl ph** Francesca Yorke; **219ar, bl, bc, & br ph** Francesca Yorke; **220–221 ph** Francesca Yorke; **223b ph** Francesca Yorke; **224 ph** Francesca Yorke; **228bl ph** Peter Cassidy; **228r ph** Francesca Yorke; **231 ph** Francesca Yorke; **232 inset ph** Francesca Yorke; **back endpaper left ph** Peter Cassidy.